TRAUMA   MATION:

A   p Guide.

By RIVKA A. EDERY, L.M.S.W.

Trauma and Transformation: A 12-Step Guide.

© 2013 by Rivka A. Edery

All rights reserved. This book, or parts thereof, may not be reproduced in any form without written permission from the author. All rights reserved.

ISBN-13: 978-1482785098

ISBN-10: 1482785099

Trauma and Transformation: A 12-Step Guide.

This book is dedicated to Goldie L., and Susan P. You extended yourself to another human being... and ended up changing the course of my life. You are the two most powerful examples of kindness, integrity, and spiritual love. My deepest gratitude to you.

Trauma and Transformation: A 12-Step Guide.

Surely goodness and mercy shall follow me all the days of

my life;

and I shall dwell in the house of the LORD forever.

Psalms 23

Trauma and Transformation: A 12-Step Guide.

ACKNOWLEDGEMENTS

I give heartfelt acknowledgement to my loving God, who has held me when I was too weak to stand; who never stopped loving me even though I could not see, hear, feel or believe it. I thank You for Your the constant gentle, unconditional presence. I want to be just like you; and while I never can, I promise to try my best to be Godly in all my ways.

...Alcoholics Anonymous World Services, Inc., for permission to use the Steps.

...Susan Price, L.M.S.W., Steven Bellew, Angela Smith, M.D., Kathryn Klingenstein, J.D., L.M.S.W., Teddy Rado, L.C.S.W.-R, James Hollywood, L.C.SW., Christopher Johnson, M.S.W., C.A.S.A.C., and Pio Cabada, L.M.S.W., R.Y.T., for your professional and personal contributions and support. You continue to be such extraordinary gifts in my life.

Trauma and Transformation: A 12-Step Guide.

... Lola S. Simmons, for being such a powerful and loyal messenger. You opened up your heart to me, and I changed because of it. You reminded me of what I have long-forgotten.

...My beloved therapist; I am who I am today, largely because of you. I will forever cherish you and our relationship.

...My sweetest, most cherished nieces and nephews for enhancing my life in ways that I can never fully express. You are each a different version of the Shechina. I love you all endlessly. Thank you so much.

...My family, including my ancestors, for instilling in me a love and reverence for books, education, and tradition.

...My friends, in and out of recovery, for your unselfish kindness, support, and friendship. Each one of you is my spiritual sister and brother.

Trauma and Transformation: A 12-Step Guide.

...Every person along my path that knowingly or unknowingly kept steering me in the right direction.

...And most of all, there would have been no growth without Goldie L., who reached out to me, offering me help in the Twelve Step program. I feel a deep love and gratitude to you for sharing your vision of healing and recovery with me. Your friendship continues to keep me strong.

Rivka A. Edery, L.M.S.W.

Trauma and Transformation: A 12-Step Guide.

CONTENTS

FORWARD	1
INTRODUCTION	7
STEP ONE: Powerlessness and unmanageability	47
STEP TWO: Who's in Charge? Issues with Authority figures	96
STEP THREE: Control, underlying issues and the need for protection	138
STEP FOUR: Secrecy, Communication and Sorting out	165
STEP FIVE: Why returning to the pain is critical to healing	207
STEP SIX: Opening the door to letting go of trauma-reactive habits	240
STEP SEVEN: Asking for help: from Victim to Survivor	288
STEP EIGHT: Preparation to Process Unfinished Business	314
STEP NINE: Unfinished Business: Responsibility vs. Self-Blame	362
STEP TEN: Every day Awareness: Body, Mind, and Soul	400
STEP ELEVEN: Attachment: From loss and disruption to Reunification	427
STEP TWELVE: Telling our story: Seeing more deeply into ourselves	449
THE TWELVE STEPS OF ALCOHOLICS ANONYMOUS	487
AFTERWARD: WHAT TO DO WITH THE PAIN OF P.T.S.D.	488
AUTHOR BIOGRAPHY	526
REFERENCE LIST	527

Trauma and Transformation: A 12-Step Guide.

DEDICATION

Every time you seek healing, you become a healer. This book is dedicated to you. Let this book serve as a candle to light your sacred path of recovery. I also dedicate this book to the world wide community of healers and researchers who care about human suffering and devote their lives to discovering the healing journey.

All my love,

Rivka A. Edery, L.M.S.W.

Brooklyn, NY

May 27, 2011

Trauma and Transformation: A 12-Step Guide.

Trauma and Transformation: A 12-Step Guide.

FORWARD

Rivka Edery is a social worker who is dedicated to helping survivors of trauma to recover healthy lives. Her book explains the invisible cord underlying the problems resulting from unresolved trauma which dramatically hinder a person trying to live a satisfying life. She clearly illustrates the therapeutic value of incorporating spirituality as part of a survivor's recovery process. This discussion is useful to both the survivor and the mental health professional.

The consequences of surviving trauma are complex, making it difficult to formulate a recovery and treatment plan. The most common defense mechanism, and the toughest one to work through, is denial. Throughout human history, lack of knowledge and non-acceptance of the perpetrators misdeeds has placed the suffering of survivors behind an armored wall, perpetuating traumatic effects. No recovery can occur behind

Trauma and Transformation: A 12-Step Guide.

this wall of forced silence, ignorance and lack of helpful resources. Over the last two decades, research has revealed the frequency of traumatic events, and their injurious effects on a survivor's psyche. Mental health professional have come to understand the connections between unresolved trauma and serious psychological problems.

The survivor's decision to begin a process of healing begins with the admission of what happened to them. This involves working through the defenses employed to shun from consciousness the excruciatingly painful memories of the traumatic events. Having passed through this phase of remembering (in any way possible), the acceptance of the truth of the traumatic experience moves the survivor towards resolution. Thus begins the creation of an internal, healing space for the survivor to feel what remained frozen in time, banished and unwelcome in consciousness. By going through the felt experience, the survivor can let go and access healing.

Trauma and Transformation: A 12-Step Guide.

The way is open to be in charge and responsible, embracing difficulties as well as personal assets and gifts.

Over the course of each survivor's life, there will be people who will criticize any efforts to acknowledge and heal from traumatic experiences. Such nay-sayers accuse survivors of using their histories to live in the past, or to make excuses for personal problems. This criticism comes from those who have limited empathy, or may be in denial about their own mistreatment. Qualified trauma specialists know that the stress from repression manifests itself in serious life difficulties. The perpetrators themselves will often intimidate their victims in an attempt to enforce silence. Although the absolute recall of traumatic events is not possible, the overwhelming consequences and burden on the untreated survivor deserves attention.

Trauma and Transformation: A 12-Step Guide.

The role of spirituality in trauma recovery is often misunderstood and subsequently minimized. It is to this need for understanding the healing potential of spirituality that *Trauma and Transformation: a 12 Step Guide* has been written. Rivka Edery informs us about the resource of spirituality while detailing the complicated puzzle of the survivor's inner reality. She illustrates how a step-by-step process of applying spiritual tools to each phase of recovery significantly alters a life of pain and confusion. She raises issues about a truly effective treatment process, showing how spiritual tools can help to surmount the challenges a survivor has to face in order to heal.

Rivka Edery takes a bold step in including a discussion directed to trauma survivors who have committed the crime of sexually abusing a minor, and who wishes to make amends. She provides a detailed discussion of this very painful and all too common problem. This serious disorder absolutely requires proper psychiatric treatment. She discusses the particular guidance needed for a perpetrator who genuinely wishes to make amends.

Trauma survivors usually have a difficult time experiencing their vulnerability and the attending feelings of having once been profoundly helpless and alone. The process of unearthing one's memories and re-experiencing anguish requires the help of skilled, knowledgeable and spiritually grounded professionals *who have done healing work on themselves.* With issues as delicate and sensitive as deep emotional wounding, each survivor and counselor must approach the recovery path with patience, self-love, self-care and the development of an appropriate support network.

The Twelve Steps comprise a spiritual program used to treat alcoholics and other individuals with a range of self destructive and addictive tendencies. *Trauma and Transformation* guides trauma survivors through the entire process of the Twelve

Steps of Alcoholic Anonymous. This powerful spiritual process is now available to help in healing the physical, mental and spiritual wounding caused by traumatic experiences. It is my hope that survivors will use this book to heal and enrich their lives in whatever way that is personally meaningful.

Angela L. Smith, M.D.

January 2013

Trauma and Transformation: A 12-Step Guide.

INTRODUCTION

This book is directed to the individuals without any experience of Twelve Step recovery, the seasoned veteran of Twelve Steps, as well as the experienced mental-health professional. The Twelve Steps of Alcoholics Anonymous have helped countless addicts. This healing process is based upon spiritual principles that speak to the human spirit. If you practice them, you *will* experience physical and spiritual growth, and emotional stability. The Twelve Steps can help you with any issues that cause emotional suffering. You can apply them to specific emotional problems, confusion, and unresolved pain. They serve as a connector to the areas in your life in which you seek self expression and fulfillment.

Consider each of the Twelve Steps as a *Power Tool* you carry around in your toolbox, for use at anytime. Steps One through Three are the "Surrender Steps", Steps Four through

Nine will heal your memories, and amazingly, they will *"clear away the wreckage of the past"*. You will also realize that due to the effects of trauma, you have misunderstood a lot about yourself, other people and the God of your understanding. As you earnestly apply these Steps to your life, you *will* get to the *truth* about yourself, other people, and the God of your understanding. All three can be distorted due to impact from trauma. It is natural to be afraid of the truth, and the fact-finding process of reaching for the truth. You will discover the joy of the truth setting you free to experiencing love and service, the most important part of this great Life Journey. And finally, Steps Ten through Twelve are about your ongoing growth, and therefore an *awakened spirit.*

The great truth about any living organism is that it is either growing or dying; there is no maintenance. This is completely true of our spiritual condition: you are always either moving towards growth, or towards regression.

Eventually, if you are open and honest with yourself, and vigorously apply these spiritual principles in your life, *spiritual laws* will begin to replace everything you have learned. A life based upon these principles will become your habit for living. If you are like most well-defended people, you may be resistant and closed-minded to any of these ideas. For you I say your ego needs to face its limitations before it can assist you in your growth. In addition, *The All Powerful Creator will not do for you what you are supposed to do for yourself.* Recovery via application of spiritual principles and concepts can be somewhat of a mystery, and there is no 'spiritual silver bullet'. The best way to start this process is to surrender to the mystery, and not try to solve it. You do not know if this program will work for you until you try it - thoroughly, honestly, and consistently.

You may find that by exploring the Twelve Steps, in the context of your traumatic history it stirs up the pot of emotions inside you. This may be a new experience in your life, which happens when you seek "conscious contact" through a spiritually sound and disciplined practice. Try to follow through with the process, and let your thoughts and feelings be as they are. If you are in the habit of fleeing from yourself, try a new way of responding and simply be with those feelings. If it touches you in some way, and you are tempted to flee from yourself, know it is the *Great Reality that Lives inside You* that is nudging you toward the pain of healing. If you learn to listen to this Voice, you will learn how to remove the blockages that prevent you from loving yourself and other people. This self-love is necessary to the process of trauma recovery. If you operate out of a *False Self*, that *False Self* will collapse by working these Twelve Steps. Every trauma survivor not only desires and needs love, yet the trauma affects your ability to give and receive love. I have applied the Twelve Steps of Alcoholics Anonymous to all areas of my life over the past sixteen years, and I have discovered they can be applied to trauma-recovery as well. People, with a history of trauma usually have a hard time facing the experience and processing it effectively. Trauma as I reference it includes early childhood victimization, traumatic events such as natural disasters, wars, and acts of terrorism, and the upheaval of divorce, accidents, and illnesses. One's stability is particularly challenged when the traumatic event has been deliberate. Particularly severe is the sexual, physical, or psychological abuse by caregivers, including harmful forms of neglect. Surviving such trauma is not an arena which one can, or should, handle alone. It calls for the knowledgeable and compassionate practice by a trained professional who, through a developed relationship with the client, will be able to skillfully take him back through the painful experience, for the purpose of healing. Our natural inclination is to shield ourselves from pain, and therefore psychological damage limits the expression of your life and depression becomes chronic.

A tenet of this book is that healing from trauma will not happen until the person has worked through the experience. The application of the Twelve Steps can greatly aide this endeavor whether the person is a child, adolescent, adult, addict, or a non-addict. Repressed traumatic experiences often cause problems later on, and in varying forms. The frightening part of processing traumatic events is the re-opening of doors to terrible places, to facilitate recovery from the original event(s). Within the context of a holding relationship that is safe, compassionate and gentle, a survivor is able to acknowledge what happened, that she survived and that she is able to live a meaningful life.

In my personal Twelve Step recovery process, I have needed a healing environment that has these components: 1) A sufficient and healthy support network, including a well-trained professional, 2) A wide range of effective recovery tools, 3) An understanding that recovery calls for a significant amount of *patience, compassion for self, time* and *energy*, 4) A willingness to approach oneself with great sensitivity and honesty concerning the realities of the traumatic events. In order to protect oneself from being overwhelmed, one must be willing to consult and learn from safe, trusted people. You cannot do this alone.

I work the Twelve Steps in my life in conjunction with a safe, well-trained therapist and a range of recovery tools. The Twelve Steps of Alcoholics Anonymous are the foundation of my recovery journey. My expectation is that the reader will carefully consider the concepts of the Twelve Steps, integrating them with their own experiences, beliefs, cultural background, and personality. These ancient, time-tested principles can become part of your personal spiritual practice.

I hope that this book can help others prepare for the process of acknowledging terrible emotional events for the purpose of healing. I believe that one's individual healing also heals others. The genuine caring of committed friends and/or professionals facilitates one's process back through the original pain, fear and hurt. This brings the greatest reward, a connection to the lost, unloved parts of you. This process has allowed me to acknowledge my losses and gains. I can feel the love that I thought could only come from someone else, and truly move on with my life. There have been many moments where this was not easy. However, when I faced the wounded, unloved parts of myself, I realized that I must love those parts to genuine acceptance.

Trauma and Transformation: A 12-Step Guide.

It is very common in recovery, to re-experience the past as the helpless, terrified person you were at the time. Along with this, is the urge to slam the door on the event, and with it, the trapped memories and buried emotions.

As you heal, your own light will shine on the paths of others on the journey. This happens because your process helps others find their truths.

As a trauma survivor who may not have any knowledge of the Twelve Steps of Alcoholics Anonymous, or as one who is in recovery, you wonder what the steps are about, and what, if any, connection they have on issues related to having survived trauma. Perhaps you may wonder what makes this book different from the vast majority of other self-help books or the existing body of Twelve Step literature. These were my own questions, and in searching for and finding my personal answers, I set them forth in the pages that follow.

What I discovered, is that by following a systemic process (steps One through Twelve), I had begun to discover my personal roadblocks, and over time, to either remove them completely, or serenely walk around them, accepting my limitations. I also uncovered my strengths, gifts and talents, all of which were once buried along with my long-forgotten history of trauma. Buried "secrets", wounds, and gifts all keep a person blocked emotionally and creatively. To my surprise, the application of the Twelve Steps of Alcoholics Anonymous helped to uncover, recover, and discover all three. With this experience, I began to discover a whole different world, and along with it, a sadness that there is so much misunderstanding, fear and ignorance regarding the Twelve Steps.

As I continue to successfully apply them to my life and assist others in doing so, I began to question if these very powerful spiritual concepts could aide in other areas of my life, specifically trauma-recovery. In my professional and personal experience, I witnessed how at the root of almost all addictive behavior there lies some long-forgotten wound(s), secret(s), and/or gift(s). Often times the gift is in a form of resiliency, chosen defense mechanisms to survive, or other expressions of creativity. I felt convinced that the power and concepts of the Twelve Steps can be appropriate for any survivor of trauma who was honest, open and willing to try this approach. I wholeheartedly trust that if they are Powerful enough to be applied to addictions, they can successfully be applied to those who survived traumatic experiences. ***My reasoning is not just based on my experience and those of others, but on the premise that addiction is one of toughest human problems to deal with, and if arrested, the original experiences can be called forth to the light and healed.***

In the pages that follow, I will introduce to you the Twelve Steps of Alcoholics Anonymous, and demonstrate how this process can help you to heal from trauma. I will share my own experience, strength and hope in applying the Twelve Steps to my own traumatic experiences, and to others I have, and continue to counsel. I will share suggestions that helped me enormously. This innovative angle is supported by a significantly more open interpretation and application of the Twelve Steps as they relate to trauma survivors. It is drawn from my personal experiences, professional work as a therapist, and the stories of an untold number of people through my sixteen years in recovery. My hope is that by applying the Twelve Steps to *Unprocessed Trauma*, you will be empowered to heal and move on with your life. Sometimes a traumatic injury results from an un-dramatic insult to the self esteem of a child, yet has profoundly limiting effects. In Twelve-Step meetings it is often said: *"identify – don't compare"*. I ask the reader to do the same.

Trauma and Transformation: A 12-Step Guide.

Trauma is defined as an emotional or psychological injury that has been caused by a deeply disturbing experience. As used in this book, "trauma" also refers to an emotional shock that is overwhelming. It can be an uncontrollable experience that shakes the person to the core. The victim repeatedly questions whether life has meaning. Such an experience can impact the survivor by creating feelings of loss of control, weakness, terror, feelings of helplessness, rage, profound loneliness, a sense of being utterly disconnected, terror of alienation, and deep vulnerability. Traumatic events might be a single event like an injury, or witnessing a violent incident. It may include several experiences, which are traumatic overall. Examples include psychological abuse, sexual abuse, incest, and exposure to violence. Trauma includes deprivation of basic needs, a prolonged divorce or custody battle, witnessing sibling abuse, witnessing domestic violence, surviving an accident, or seeing people killed or injured during war. The effects of the latter are apparent in the current high rate of suicide among our returning soldiers. It also can be traumatic to be shamed at school, mistreated by a sadistic teacher, forced into injurious sports, and pushed aside due to family upheaval, such as moving or the death of a parent.

BRIEF DESCRIPTION OF ALCOHOLICS ANONYMOUS

Since 1939 when the Twelve Steps were organized and adopted by Alcoholics Anonymous, numerous self-help groups, treatment centers, and individuals, have been guided and supported on their recovery journey by applying the steps to their lives. The power of the steps lie in the practical, spiritual and emotional resources to facilitate recovery from alcoholism, sexual compulsions, gambling, eating disorders, internet addiction, and more.

The experience, strength and hope of those that have applied the steps to their life, speak to the certainty of their power. Conversely, it is imperative to acknowledge that the Steps were authored by men predominantly for their needs in recovery, at a time when there was little known about trauma and its effects.

We now know from seventy four years of experience and knowledge with the Twelve Step recovery process, that healing may imply something different for survivors of trauma. Furthermore, the journey of healing is very different for each person: "working" the Steps is certainly not a black and white process.

As you explore the in-depth meaning of the steps while reading this book and connect to your own history of traumatic events, you will experience feelings, memories, and beliefs, which can also be referred to as your *True Self*. This continues to be my definition of recovery; my journey of being restored to integrity. The goal of healing from trauma is to unify your inner and outer life, and each of the steps serves as a guide in self-honesty and soul-searching. The ultimate theme of the steps is to connect with your True Self and live a life that is meaningful, free from bondage of the past. I view the Twelve Steps as *Twelve Lamps*, each shedding light toward a meaningful life, free from unnecessary pain and suffering, filled with hope and possibility.

As you turn towards the part of you that has been hurt, you will need to be gentle and compassionate. Since the Steps were formulated by men in 1939 for alcoholics, the language and structure of the steps can seem dated and even intimidating. I hope to carry you beyond some of the stilted language to the profound usefulness of these spiritual principles.

Trauma and Transformation: A 12-Step Guide.

Many trauma survivors have no desire to explore their experiences. The most obvious reason is the fear of re-experiencing the pain, suffering, and loss of control. Another common reason is not feeling or believing that one has been affected at all, or that anything can really help. If you are nodding your head in agreement as you read this, I ask you not to close the book just yet. Allow yourself the space to explore how the steps might apply to your specific issues and to you as a person. You will find that I speak more directly to the ways in which a trauma survivor looking at the steps might feel resistance to exploring each step. As has been said many times, beneath the archaic wording of the Steps, is a potent energy that is best understood when experienced personally. My personal journey is a testament to this. I continue to travel through the steps, and in doing so, feel called upon to share how the wisdom, energy, and power of the steps can help you to transform your painful experiences. I do not write as a voice of authority, but of a deeply grateful traveler along the path of recovery. Step Twelve calls for an awakening, and for keeping it by giving it away. I hope that this book, in some way, accomplishes that.

In order to have a discussion on trauma and healing, you must first and foremost, feel that your experience has been properly understood. In his poem *"Song of Man"*, the great Lebanese poet and philosopher, Kahlil Gibran, writes:

> *"I suffered at the hands of despotic rulers;*
> *I suffered slavery under insane invaders;*
> *I suffered hunger imposed by tyranny;*
> *Yet, I still possess some inner power*
> *With which I struggle to greet each day.*
> *My mind is filled, but my heart is empty;*
> *My body is old, but my heart is an infant.*
> *Perhaps in youth my heart will grow, but I*
> *Pray to grow old and reach the moment of*
> *My return to God. Only then will my heart fill!"* [1]

Surviving trauma, psychologically, physically, and emotionally, can feel similar to the words of this poet. Often

---

[1] Gibran, Kahlil. *The Treasured Writings of Kahlil Gibran*, (New York: Castle Books, 2010), 57.

survivors will speak of emptiness, a silent wound, and yearning to "*go home*". It can also feel very isolating to have the feelings you thought were gone and done with, creep up in you suddenly, and without cause. It can feel like agonizing torture when you are triggered, especially in the silence of the night. I am also mystified at the resiliency of the human spirit, and how that "inner power" that the poet refers to, still remains with some people, even after having undergone a traumatic experience(s). I continue to be amazed at how some survivors can genuinely extend warmth, compassion and kindness when they themselves were denied it. In contrast, those people that were not traumatized often seem to lack in these precious qualities.

It is this mysterious aspect of the human condition, why certain people, denied love and compassion and having experienced some form of trauma, have the ability to heal, love and inspire... while others do not. The subject of trauma is a grim one and one that makes a sensitive soul cry out in despair. The courage to investigate one's own story creates the possibility of really getting to know the lost or disowned parts of oneself. "Lost or disowned" is that part of your life which due to experiencing trauma, you do not want to have anything more to do with.

I believe that every man, woman and child desire to experience life without closed doors; a life led by a glorious and free heart. I also believe that included in this wish, is the desire to really love oneself. As such, recovery can apply to anyone who remains honest, open, and willing to grow. It may seem like a treacherous affair to inquire into one's traumatic past. Having the hope that you will experience healing and integrity by doing this can seem like a far-fetched idea, not worth the effort. Healing and integrity are a consequence of relating to oneself as one would in a close relationship with their beloved. However, as long as you stay away from the locked door of forbidden emotions, unprocessed memories, and unnecessary guilt, there will be the sentry of the Unhealthy Ego standing in front of the forbidden door, forever guarding its contents fiercely.

Of course not everyone experiences trauma in the same way, or the same kind of trauma, as it exists on a continuum.

However, by definition, a traumatic experience creates some kind of disturbance, and it is a wound that requires the balm of understanding and compassion. The key in this process lays in the application of spiritual principles, as a part of integrating mind, body, and soul healing. As you deepen your understanding and acceptance of yourself, learn how to have healthy relationships with people, and give back in service, the circle of recovery is complete. It is my experience and those of countless others, that applying the Twelve Steps greatly aides in this process. Sadly, there is much room for ignorant interpretation of recovery, faulty belief, and "projection" of our negative experiences. This can happen in any situation, and the Twelve Steps of Alcoholics Anonymous are no different. For example, I erroneously believed that for me to properly work the steps, it would involve continued self-blame and submission to an authority figure, referenced as "God". It is with the processing of my own authority figure issues, that I saw the faulty belief operating. As others continue to share their experience, strength and hope, I am able to blend theirs, with my own emerging consciousness, and in the process have found, and continue to live from my True Self.

However, this achievement did not come easy for me. There were many times that I danced around the idea of recovery "not having anything in it for me," that it was possibly dogmatic, or not effective. Many times I have felt that the process was boring, frightening or out of date for my needs. As these feelings rose from my depths as a scared child, they fell on the ears of loving, spiritual people who never chastised me and encouraged me to stay on the path. On a number of occasions I have flirted with the idea of quitting altogether, but my overpowering yearning to prevent my Soul from drowning, gave me the courage to carry on. Many times I have faced the frozen feelings buried down in the depths of my unconscious, which emerged to seek my attention. I did not think that I could survive a face-to-face encounter with my sleeping ghosts, and I had no idea what could have possibly awoken them from their slumber. As my heart was heavy from being flamed in agony, I desperately sought for meaning in all of this.

I discovered that the personal meaning for me was a rising of consciousness. I found that during moments when I felt most weary, the safe releasing was actually the crux of my liberty. I also found that the unconditional love of people in my support network, including my therapist, felt powerful enough to dispel the terrifying grip that these feelings had on me. Through time, patience and great compassion, I was slowly learning and incorporating what I was freely receiving, and applying it to reprogram certain parts of me so that I could be the parent I had longed for. I was creating a safe emotional space inside of me, and this space has now become my spiritual home. This spiritual home inside me is enabled by having a unified self. This unity was not something I ever dreamed possible, as I once knew nothing of even having lost and frozen parts of me. I learned that when you give yourself the space to cry, laugh, and express yourself as naturally as a child, you speak the language of the heart. And it is *this* language that has restorative power. After many years in recovery, I can now comprehend that my tears, silence, creative process, words and actions, have all given birth to my personal transformation.

Trauma and Transformation: A 12-Step Guide.

In the beginning of my journey I carried the wounds of traumatic betrayal; acts that were deliberately inflicted upon me at a tender age. I did not care for, nor seek on a conscious level, to secure a truthful and loving relationship with myself. In all the hours I have devoted to the pursuit of finding and loving my Soul, I can joyfully state that this love I now feel for myself is worth the years of dedicated work on this path. I have gone from feeling very frightened, weak, and disconnected, to feeling content, confident and whole. There are still moments when I feel imprisoned behind my old fears, beliefs and faulty logic, and this is a part of being human. I have let go of my once-ambitious aim to eradicate these completely. My goal now is to remain my own best friend. This is accomplished through my actions, words, deeds, thoughts, and in giving back. Even during the moments when the ghosts of the past come to pay their respects, I am comforted in the knowledge that I will never, ever be shackled again in the way I once was. The inspiration of millions in recovery that have gone before me, and that travel with me, continues to fill my inner lamp.

When I had begun to apply the steps to my Wound of Trauma, I did not know what lay ahead or if there was any real purpose in doing so. I just knew that I was feeling more and more ready to open the door, which until a certain point, was very tightly guarded. My heart has since been purified by the tears of flaming sorrow that I have shed over the blindness of those that hurt me, and their gross misuse of power. In hindsight, I see how valuable this experience has been for me, because without spending the time lamenting and mourning what was stolen from me - without this grief work - my heart could not be illuminated by Love. My brilliant therapist would tell me that when memories and feelings remain buried, so do the gifts.

However, I experienced some challenges along the way. There was often an empty lure that drew me to seek a false refuge, so that I could escape from my traumatic experiences. I was vulnerable to seeking relief in false ways. When I sought such a false refuge, the feelings that ensued felt like I was imprisoned in chains of pain. When I learned and practiced to ask for help from safe others, and shared in an emotionally honest way, I became less and less afraid of this vulnerability. This freedom to share myself in an emotionally honest way continues to bring me closer to my own truth. I had always wanted to share on this level, but did not know how. I learned to take risks, to try out the process, honor my journey, pursue a spiritual life, and to avoid counterfeit love at all costs. It is so common to seek counterfeit love when one is always 'on the run' emotionally. This is typical behavior for those with unprocessed trauma and grief. You do not naturally turn to spiritual principles when it is so much easier to avoid, distract, or ignore those feelings all together.

I learned over time to enrich my own heart with *my* love, which I seemed to be able to generously extend to others. I have since taken on the spiritual discipline of paying close attention to how I speak to myself, to the company that I keep, and to attentive self-care. This process continues to deepen and evolve in conjunction to the efforts that I extend to my spiritual practice.

I relish a lifestyle of loving compassion for the child I once was. This is the foundation of my recovery. Through working the Twelve Steps, I have grown to honor, love, and respect the person I was created to be. I believe that it is my Creator's Will for me to be in recovery. Knowing nothing of this path, I felt chosen by it! This highlights the reality that as human beings, we not only long for our basic human needs for food and shelter, but for a self that is unified and loved. I am fascinated by where this urge takes some of us. There is a vast amount of literature with experts of every persuasion, providing so many different perspectives and ideas on recovery and healing from trauma. There will not likely be a shortage of authorities or laypeople ready to find reasonable explanations and options for all observed symptoms and solutions for this brand of suffering. And yet there are moments, when you get brief glimpses into the profound nature of your own suffering, and fear that recovery is not possible.

True recovery is dynamic, and yet there will be frustrating, disappointing moments which feel like set-backs, but are, in fact, a necessary part of *"peeling away the layers of the onion"*. Those moments reveal to you where your vulnerability lies, what feelings you would rather not face, and where your' greatest hope in freedom lies. I view our gifts as Angels, and our demons as the unforgiving parts of us. These are real. For many who have undergone a trauma, it is hard to believe in, and integrate, all of this. For many trauma survivors, living can feel like it is defined by society's dictates, economics, politics and fear of breaking down the walls of our unremembered stories. And yet, an instinct and ability for healing persists, not just on a biological level, but on a psychic level as well. You maintain a conviction that not everything in your life should be controlled by the faulty lessons you learned in childhood. This has helped me understand my unique spiritual challenges.

Through modern psychology, much has been discovered about healing and recovery on a biological and emotional level. But there remains a mysterious element to the healing process. The healing of psychic wounds does not occur in a linear, obvious way, and is exquisitely unique to the individual. In view of the various types of mental and emotional disorders, I have asked if spiritual principles can be affective if applied to trauma (usually at the root of these disorders), and what is the identified relationship between these principles along the psychic and the physical continuum. Although healing psychic wounds and their relationship to spiritual concepts cannot be scientifically proven, it also has not, and cannot, be proven invalid. From my observations, it seems like some people may have a natural propensity for this type of healing, while others do not. Many factors account for this. Common sense does not require you to accept the mysterious, the uncommon, or whatever else does not fit your schema. Should you not abandon your usual ideas of what is worth pursuing? As you tune in to the echo of un-cried tears, unspoken words, unfulfilled dreams, unhealed pain, must you follow the idea that spirituality heals some forms of human suffering? Cannot existing treatment modalities such as Cognitive Behavioral Therapy, be effective and be enough? Must there be a place for the Twelve Steps written by men, predominantly for alcoholics over half a century ago, in the realm of trauma recovery? Can spiritual energy and principle make themselves manifest in ways not always physically observable? These questions and my own healing have opened the door to the intriguing world of psychic healing. I have always been fascinated with these questions.

Throughout my years in recovery, I have documented my thoughts, feelings, moods, unexplained coincidences, dreams, and experiences. I have read numerous books on this subject, sought a professional degree and license, and attended trainings, workshops and conferences on the subject. I have spent many hours conversing with others on this topic, both in and out of Twelve Step meetings. All that I have gathered suggests for me that the miracle of recovery; its mysterious dimension, and the unknowable facets, have always been real, accessible, and potent for anyone, *if and only if*, they are capable of being honest with themselves.

Recovery is truly a personal process, and some aspects of it defy rational explanation. But the final analysis suggests that the human mind, body and the Soul working in unison have supernatural capabilities. In recovery you do not just treat one facet of the human being: it is the trinity of Mind, Body and Soul. This very relationship has a profound effect on you. Some people will propose that this is not as true as you think or that it is unscientific. Simply put, the stories, ideas, and discussion in this book means that what I know of myself and my ability to heal my own psychic wounds, represents only a peek of how things really are. I extend this belief to others as well.

The question remains for the reader: how can the people with no history or knowledge of trauma, or recovery, evaluate what they read in this book? There is no scientific criterion to be applied or established here. I therefore suggest that you read with an open mind and relate back to yourself what rings true; what you connect to. I can never testify that my personal experiences will apply to someone else. This is impossible to establish and is not the way it works. I also want to reiterate that feelings stemming from severe trauma, traumatic terror, etc, are best processed with a safe and well-trained professional. I do not suggest that you attempt to do such work alone, without safe people to guide and support your journey. If you choose to simply read this book, and not apply any of the material to your own history, you may discover that certain difficult feelings may emerge. Should this occur, please seek the appropriate help – **you do not have to go through this alone**. Traumatic terror, rage, and pain require a safe holding space, a strong foundation in some kind of support network. I also suggest to you dear reader, that you begin to document your journey. This includes your personal efforts, experiences, coincidences, progress, and your process in general.

Throughout human history, people have documented the phenomenon they experienced at the specific time and place they were in, and some of this has helped humanity to advance in some way. It is the same principle on an individual basis. You are your own best witness, and although you may doubt or disbelieve your traumatic experience(s), you will find many "witnesses" that can validate your personal pain and story. But even when you find such people, you may also get disappointed that their shortcomings prevent them from fully grasping what you went through. You may agree that certain things you survived still remain hidden from your conscious mind, and you yourself may not fully grasp what you went through.

I have put in an extensive effort to *fully* uncover my childhood history and the attending feelings, memories and unresolved issues. I see now that this is not possible, and not necessary for psychic healing. It is not possible for any kind of intervention or therapeutic method, to erase all of the painful, negative programming so many of you are given by your life experiences. Even after a hundred years of therapy, and extensive knowledge in the field of mental health, you cannot ever completely erase the effects of trauma, or fully recover every painful memory. But what you can have is the experience and understanding that certain treatment methods work for you, and some do not.

For me, applying the Twelve Steps, coupled with weekly therapy, and other tools, as the foundation of my journey, continues to work for me. It truly does take an open mind to let go of the notion that there is the possibility that one size fits all, and that there exists the perfect method that will work for anyone who survived trauma. Recovery is a delicate art. It was only when I opened myself up to this sensitive art, that I was able to receive the critical self-knowledge and subsequent release of buried gifts. In essence, I aligned with the forces of healing, and I believe in everyone's ability to do the same. As the saying goes, *"what does not come from the heart, does not reach the heart"*, and I very much want to reach you, so I will speak from my heart. I ask that you listen to my message in this book, with your heart.

The following is a poem that I wrote when I had first begun to wake up to my own Creativity.

Gifted Healer,

Why do you weep? Do not despair. You are not without a purpose.
My hands are constantly over your head praying for you. I bless you constantly.
We have been travelling together all along. You just weren't ready to notice me.
I love you.
The Energy is always with you. It will not leave you.
Do not be afraid, because you are not alone. It's the Souls of thousands who have been on the very same road
You travel on, that accompany you.
The beautiful colors are all around you. I see them all the time. Soon, you will too.
I shine My Beauty and Light upon your head for all the days of your life.
I can always see those stunning crystals and light circling your heart.
Will you let me dry your tears?

Place your weary head on my shoulder.
My arms are strong enough to hold you until you are ready to let go.
Your tears break my heart, and when you smile the tears of the Angels dry up.
In your dedication to keep on trying, you inspire countless Souls you have never met.
Do not suffer in fear of being rejected. You are a part of the forces of Love.
You are always worthy. You are always blessed.
How comforted I am by your presence. Your heartbeat quiets my fears inside.
Open your heart and have fun discovering the jewels inside!
And when you are ready, go on and share them with those that have eyes to see.
Gifted Healer, how I long to hold you! Come forward and trust me.
Trust the Energy that drew us together. (-R.A. Edery, 2-21-09).

Before you begin to read and practice the exercises in this book, please take a moment now to describe in one or two paragraphs, your concept of *"spiritual awakening"*.

Afterwards, please continue reading.

_____

_____

_____

_____

Trauma and Transformation: A 12-Step Guide.

STATEMENT OF INTENT

Each survivor is unique and each survivor's experiences are unique. You deserve to receive the right kind of help in healing from the trauma(s) you experienced. The ideas, stories, suggestions and information presented in this book are not a substitute for, nor a form of, psychotherapy. Please seek help from a competent professional if you are experiencing symptoms of trauma, or if you decide to follow the exercises suggested in this book, and you feel overwhelmed by your reactions.

STEP ONE

We admitted we were powerless over alcohol - that our lives had become unmanageable.

Step One is your guide on how to process and heal from trauma. It will also serve as your guide to personal growth, which is applicable for anyone, not just for trauma survivors. Why is processing trauma, and personal growth, important for you? You may wonder of the necessity of going through such a process, especially if you are high functioning and successful in life. After all, growing pains are indeed painful, and we humans are wired to avoid pain and seek pleasure. You also have a responsibility to take care of yourself, and although *some* pain *can be* avoided, there is the pain that cannot be avoided, and requires processing. This is your turn now, and you begin with this first step. The word "*admit*" is to accept what is valid and true for you personally. This step asks you to accept what areas in your life that have been affected by your personal trauma history, causing your life to be out of control, unsatisfying, or chronically problematic for you.

Since you do not hear answers until you ask the question, I am going to get you started on your journey by suggesting the following exercise: set aside a quiet and comfortable space, free from distractions. I am going to ask you to answer four critical questions. Take a few moments first to get relaxed and comfortable, taking several deep breaths. You may want to say a prayer, recite a poem or do any self-soothing activity to center yourself. My favorite prayer, which I adapted from one heard in the Twelve Step rooms is:

"Dear Higher Power, please help me in setting aside everything I think I know about myself, my traumatic experiences, the Steps, Spirituality, and especially You, God. I pray that I may

have a truly open mind, so that I may have a new experience with these things. Please help me see the truth. AMEN."

When you feel ready, write down your answers to the following four questions:

Question 1): What part(s) of your life do you find most difficult to remember? (These can be a specific age, location where you lived, series of events, time period, etc).

_____

_____

_____

_____

Question 2): If you were to write a complete account of your entire life, from beginning to the present moment, which parts of your life would, you either skip over entirely, or write very little about? (These would be the parts of your story that if you could change what happened, you would do so without hesitation. These are the parts that awaken the deepest feelings of shame, fear, pain, disgust, anger, or of isolation. They cause you to either feel flooded with intense emotions, or to feel emotionless, numb, blocked, or a strong revulsion by them).

_____

_____

_____

_____

Question 3): Do you have a pattern of specific themes in nightmares, flashbacks, painful physical sensations (that are without medical explanation), dysfunctional behaviors, relationship patterns, or personal escape mechanisms that are destructive?

_____

_____

_____

_____

Question 4): Do you doubt that *you* can be happy, joyous, serene, and psychologically free, no matter what you went through, and how you feel about it?

_____

_____

_____

_____

Take some time now to review your answers, paying very close attention to the sensations in your body, and the emotions which you are feeling now. Is there any acknowledgment (*"to admit"*) that you were unable to have produced any effect on your situation(s) whatsoever (*"powerless"*), and that because of those parts of your story (that you would rather avoid entirely), some of your human affairs (your life) are lacking in control ("*unmanageable*")? If you answered in the affirmative, you as a trauma survivor have just conceded to your Innermost Self (your heart), that you were powerless, during the traumatic event, and after the event. And perhaps even years after the event(s), your life had become unmanageable because of your Spiritual condition (an after-effect of what you survived). After this exercise, I suggest that you pause and say out loud, or meditate in your heart the following: "*Heal in me what needs to be healed. Reveal in me what needs to be revealed*".

If you are like most people, you may have been raised in a dysfunctional home environment and/or community. In addition, if you survived any traumatic events, you probably have a distorted blueprint of living, of what is "normal", healthy, and functional. It is also likely that you have experienced, on some level, a form of emotional slavery in your life, as a result of your upbringing and environment. For example, if you thought, or still think, that you have control over people (i.e., and your reactions, internal or external, can influence others) this is a classic form of emotional slavery, and your area of powerlessness. You are therefore dependent on others for you to feel a certain way. By taking this first step, you begin the process of unlearning a core dysfunctional belief that no doubt, has influenced your many interactions and relationships.

It is not your fault that you developed self-limiting attitudes as a result of what you survived, and you will now be able to outgrow what is not serving you well in life. Emotional growth includes freedom from a sense of false control and dependency, not avoiding what needs your attention, outgrowing your unhealthy fears, replacing unproductive physical and emotional defenses, false beliefs, and ending spiritual isolation. At this point, you may be thinking the following: *"Just get over it and move on! If I dwell on it, talk about it, explore it, I will just make it worse. I don't know why I should bother with this healing stuff? After all, look at how "fine" I am without knowing or dealing with happened!"* Perhaps you have convinced yourself that avoidance is the answer to helplessness and loneliness that often accompanies surviving trauma.

Step One is a great challenge, because it requires a survivor to face the reality that you were once truly powerless over something utterly overwhelming and disruptive to your life (*trauma*). If there was a time in your life where powerlessness and natural dependency was used against you (childhood abuse and trauma), you may be highly triggered by "admitting powerlessness" over what happened. After all, when you are powerless over something, it implies that you did not do something, but rather, you get done to. If your powerlessness was once a weapon used to control you, and your protesting what happened carried little weight, you may associate "powerlessness" with defenseless, and this can be entirely too painful. You may have never taken the risk to feel this vulnerable, or to explore the definitions of these terms, as it pertains to your *growth*. After all, most people have the need to be in control, let alone if believing you are in control once saved your life, your mind, your sanity, etc.

If you work on Step One, you may come face to face to how emotionally frozen you are in certain areas (unresolved, unprocessed trauma), and may fear that you will not be able to stand the pain. For some people, feelings are like a faucet that you can turn on, or off, but that there is only one valve, titled "**Feelings**". If this valve is turned off, you may feel you exist in a state of emotional numbness or disconnect from yourself. A clinical term for this is *"isolation of affect"*, and this occurs when the emotions 'freeze' because they were once too painful to feel. It is a painful experience when you turn the faucet on: the water (feelings) may just drip very slowly, or it may gush out, out of control. You may feel convinced that if this happens, you will lose your mind, or go crazy. (As I frequently mention throughout this book, please seek professional help if you need to. This inner work requires the right kind of support - do not think that you need to handle all this on your own).

As I previously mentioned, if you grew up in a dysfunctional home and/or community, you were not presented with a blueprint of healthy, functional ways of responding, reacting, behaving, or managing your emotions. This is why it's very important to **_unlearn_** what is not true and not healthy. You may have been forced to remain unaware of the trauma, and to remain in an emotionally frozen (numb) state.

Some survivors over-react and harm themselves or others. In either case, there are always the elements of either over-reacting or under-reacting. You do not have to remain this way the rest of your life. The opposite of Step One, is the erroneous and *highly misleading* belief that you have power (over what happened; people, places, and things), which results in you taking inappropriate or excessive responsibility. This is because you think that you can stop the person(s), or event(s), or that in some way **_you_** actually caused it to happen. Human nature is such that people would rather feel **_guilty_** than **_powerless._** That is why you assume a great deal of power; to counteract the real feelings of powerlessness, which is inherent in having been traumatized. In what areas of your life can you see evidence for this? Take a few minutes now to write how this is true for you.

_____

_____

_____

_____

> **TIP:** Whenever you feel miserable, consider if it may be because you are forgetting that you are powerless of the situation (people, place, or thing), and you are mentally trying to change someone or something else, that you do not have any power to change.

> **TIP:** Being powerless does NOT mean you are helpless. *It just means that you must change your source of power. You are not the Source.* Internally, you may have taken on the entire burden, which leads to emotional entrapment and a form of mental slavery. Unlearning your original beliefs about power, and responsibility, is the essence of Step One.

> **TIP:** Step One will allow you the freedom to love people in a genuine way, because you will be free of needing anything from them. By letting go of control and manipulation, both you and the other person are free to be who they are. You allow yourself, and others, to experience love on a different level – free from demands and hidden agendas.

Let's take a look at your personal trauma story, and explore the significance and impact that Step One will have one your life. If you have read this far, perhaps you are wondering if something you went through, but have not dealt with properly, is making your life unmanageable in some way. If you are like most people, you may think that you are in complete control of yourself, your feelings, and behavior. Therefore, you may not have any reason to re-visit the event(s). You may be afraid of buried feelings such as fear, rage, pain, sadness, grief, self-doubt, self-blame, confusion and a sense of isolation and separateness.

To admit that you were once completely powerless over what happened automatically strips you of any long-held core belief that you are in control. The need for holding on to such a belief is because of the false sense of safety and security it provides. Such a belief also helps you to keep the doubt and blame away, even if it is only on a superficial level. You may also not want to admit that you were once powerless of what happened, if you see yourself as someone that can handle any circumstance or feeling. For some people, always being in control is a way of preventing rejection or humiliation. If you are one of those people, you may think that this is what life is about.

Another major fear in admitting that you were once powerless over what happened is because you translate that as to mean that you are now giving up control for someone else to be in control. This step, however, is really about the choice to look at your powerlessness as part of the process of wound-cleansing. The wound is the traumatic event(s), and the cleansing is addressing and replacing, your undercurrent of emptiness, unmet needs, pain, anger and fear, or anything that is a recurrent, negative influence on your life. If it meets this description, mostly likely it keeps your life unmanageable in some way for you.

The way that this undercurrent is addressed (cleansing of wounds), must begin with admitting that your emotional, spiritual, and psychological wounding needs to be honored. You honor your wounding by cleansing the poison, and placing soothing ointment and protection on top of the wound. This is the process of being restored to wholeness (sanity). When you start with "admission" of powerlessness, you can finally give up control of what you had no control over: people, places, things and events that *you did not cause*. For some trauma survivors, Step One is totally logical. You cannot control what happened to you, your reactions or your feelings around this issue. It may be obvious to certain individuals that living a life with such buried pain requires the proper intervention. Those individuals may not have resistance to Step One.

If this is the first time you are really considering this idea, you may experience this as very comforting, scary and/or intensely powerful. To admit that you were once powerfulness over the actions of others in your life, which were traumatic for you, is reassuring and comforting. You will now understand why all your attempts to understand the events, or behavior of the people involved, minus the acknowledgment that you were not responsible, had not worked. If you were once unable to control someone else's harmful behavior, the inherent meaning of this, is that you were not responsible for what happened. And if you really get it that you were not responsible, it will be much easier for you to practice responding to situations that trigger you, instead of reacting.

You pay a high emotional price if you go through life blaming yourself for your suffering, when you are not to be blamed. This makes you very susceptible to reacting, instead of responding appropriately to whatever it going on. Although these words are easy to read on a page, I learned it slowly and painfully, incident by incident, until I was able to put this concept into practice.

The application of Step One in your life is that your personal acceptance that you had no power over people's wrong, inappropriate and hurtful actions creates the space for you to finally start making sense of the pain and/or problems in your life. Your understanding of Step One, at this point, may give you a glimmer of hope that perhaps *you can finally let go of that emotional burden you are carrying.* What a relief! The other side of this coin is that if you are miserable, perhaps you are focusing on something that is not an available option.

Take a moment now to reflect on how this may be true in your life right now. Remember that you are entirely responsible for **_your_** behavior, regardless of what you went through, so make sure to be honest with yourself.

Trauma and Transformation: A 12-Step Guide.

_____

_____

_____

_____

It is to be expected that at the very beginning of your process in exploring and re-visiting what happened to you, you will feel various intense emotions. A part of the intensity is the response to once having been so powerless, and you having to deal with the attending consequences of the traumatic experiences. If you have shame linked to what happened, you will probably feel significant resistance to acknowledging it. You may also not feel ready to sit with the feelings that come up. There are those people that are incredibly well-defended against such pain. They "forgot" about it altogether and feel that the trauma had no effect on them. If this describes you, Step One will be particularly challenging.

It is human nature for a person to feel threatened and highly uncomfortable when seeing themselves without personal power or control. If you are like most people, you prefer to have more control over your life, and not less. This applies to most people, and is not exclusive to survivors of trauma. Seeking to have more control is especially applicable to you if you intimately know the meaning of losing control and being powerless when you are vulnerable.

You may still be wondering, at this point, how the Twelve Steps of Alcoholics Anonymous, and this step specifically, is going to help you, if you survived a traumatic event(s). Since you are asking the question, this step has an amazing answer for you. It is only when you really understand that you cannot control what was done to you, by no fault of your own, that you find a way to let go of the burden. By letting go of the false belief that you could have done something to change what happened you finally take the first step on this journey towards healing.

THE ORIGINAL CLASSROOM OF CONTROL

If you have issues of control, you most likely learned it in the infamous Classroom of Childhood. Your childhood is the original classroom where you learn and develop your core beliefs which may include the strong and false belief that you have power over others. From the classroom of childhood, throughout your life, you carry and apply all your beliefs wherever you go. If you are carriers of the belief that you can control other people, you are carriers of something that is at best, an illusion and at worst is highly destructive. If you want to stop believing in your illusion of control and start acknowledging your powerlessness, take a close look at what exactly you survived.

Take a moment right now to answer the following two questions, which will help you reflect on the origin of control issues:

1) Where you ever in situations where there was an unfair imbalance of power?

_____

_____

_____

_____

2) Referring to the situation you just detailed, did you really have any influence in the situation?

_____

_____

_____

_____

GUILT AND SHAME AS CHIEF OPERATORS IN CONTROL

The following is written by Ken Keyes, Jr., and what I find to be a powerful description of the role of guilt and shame with issues of control.

> *I hide **IT**...*
> ***IT** must be important...*
> *If **IT** is important, I must protect **IT**...*
> *To protect **IT**, I must keep others away...*
> *To keep others away, I must hide **MYSELF**...*
> *I wish I knew why I felt so alone....* [2]

Take some time now to answer the following six questions:

1) What comes up for you immediately when reading this? (Pay attention to physical sensations, feelings, images, thoughts, etc).

---

[2] Keyes, Jr. Ken. *Gathering Power Through Insight and Love.* (Coos Bay, Oregon: Living Love Publications, 1987), Pg. 148.

Trauma and Transformation: A 12-Step Guide.

_____

_____

_____

_____

2) Everyone has an "*IT*" - what is yours?

_____

_____

_____

_____

3) What if other's found out the answer you put in Question 2? How would that impact your way of operating emotionally?

_____

_____

_____

_____

4) After evaluating your answer in Question 3, can you self-identify a more compassionate view towards yourself?

_____

_____

_____

_____

5) Do you yearn for healing in this area?

_____

_____

_____

_____

6) Even if you don't feel "life is unmanageable", can you describe what your life would be like if "*IT*" was no longer a secret? Elaborate as much as you can.

_____

_____

Trauma and Transformation: A 12-Step Guide.

_____

_____

You hide the pain from yourself or try to forget, or try to feel better, in order to change the original feelings of what happened. But such "forgetting" is only temporary and reality quickly returns when you are triggered (emotional displacement) in some way by what happened. Here is how my friend Adam put it:

"When I was a child, my father would beat me regularly, usually in alcoholic stupors. He would attack me mercilessly. I was terrified of him. Every day when I would come home from school I would cautiously approach the house, and when he wasn't home I would breathe a huge sigh of relief. When he was home, I would try to appease him, convince him not to hurt me, avoid him as much as possible, and often just pray he would ignore me. Sometimes, he would actually listen to me,

mumble something under his breath, and walk away. At a tender age, I was convinced that I possessed a huge power over other people, because after all, my father was my universe, and this must be because I am in his way. But as I got older, and without knowledge there was a possibility of any connection, I confessed to my best friend that I was having significant control issues in relationships. For example, if my friends, co-workers or partner was in a bad mood, or having a bad day, I automatically assumed and believed that I was the guilty party. This was a terrifying experience for me, and it happened all the time! I hated living this way, but I had no clue how to change this. The pain and stress was unmanageable in the deepest sense of the word. I desperately wanted out of this pain, so I took the risk of taking step one, as a starting point. After all, what was there to lose, besides just a few dysfunctional beliefs? That would be nice..."

For Adam, this kind of trauma was not something he consciously chose to remember. He did not feel he had to admit he was powerless over his father, since he actually thought, at times, that he had power over him (in a negative way). He also did not think it was even "that bad" until he felt he could no longer live with such an emotional roller coaster of anxiety and the state of isolation that this drove him to. When he began to explore what happened, how horrible of a life he had living with *"that mean drunk"*, and how his illusions of control affected his life, he got in touch with the original pain, which up until now, had been buried and stuck. Now when he gets triggered, his Step One Affirmation is the following: *"This may not be in my plan, but I can get through it"*. He finds this simple statement an effective reminder that there are things that he can do nothing about, and sometimes a simple prayer is far more dignifying than getting in the boxing ring with someone.

There is also another facet of the control you learned early in life, and that is to bottle up what you felt. There is a Buddhist saying, that I mention several times throughout the book that states: *"Whatever you run from will chase you. Whatever you chase will run away from you"*. If you try to control your feelings, it will gain control over you, and in turn, you attempt to control other people's feelings, something that is not at all possible! This is one common example of unmanageability. You chase a shadow of illusion (something that is not there but appears to be real), and in this chase, you create for yourself an endless loop of control and unmanageability.

Perhaps on some level you know that no matter how you desperately wish a traumatic event did not happen, you know that you cannot change the past, your original feelings and reactions, and that how you felt and reacted *was your truth*. This is your most real part of yourself, and by exploring this buried truth, you can let go of all of the manifestations of your attempts to do away with it. My friend Daniel shared with me his personal traumatic experience:

> "I could never please my clinically depressed mother. No matter what I said or did, she either ignored me completely or compulsively raged at me. That was the nature of her relationship with me. Her rages were deeply terrifying and out of control. I was always trying to placate her, never could say what I was really feeling and thinking, and learned that being honest and fulfilling my needs was "bad". It was dangerous to be around her. During my marriage I operated from this place of hiding and fear. I was always trying to please and placate my partner, at the expense of being myself. I wasn't myself, because I did not know how, and my fear of rejection and abandonment, was a gaping wound that was controlling me! When I began exploring my mother's treatment of me, I got in touch

with the frozen grief. I cried in therapy and on the kind shoulders of the men in my support group. Although frightening at first, it was what I had always longed for: to cry on someone's shoulder. I just never thought that was acceptable or "manly" – to have feelings and express them in a genuine way. When I opened up this wound, I uncovered sexual abuse by my maternal uncle, and this fact-finding process took my recovery to a whole new level. I suddenly couldn't tolerate hiding my feelings. I felt I awakened on a whole different level. But it began with one simple, bold, courageous step: As a child, I could not possess any power over what was done to me. Not any of it. As an adult in my marriage and other friendships, I chose over and over again to express myself in a real, honest and kind way. This is how I "work" this step in my life. I hope others can find the same relief."

You cannot overpower a traumatic event, and other people are beyond your power to control. This is the essence of Step One. If you integrate this principle into the very fiber of your being, you are experiencing the power of Step One. You may need to return to this step as often as you need to, and feel free to do so. It is now that you stand a real chance in changing your self-identified unhealthy patterns. Let's try this out. Close your eyes, take a few deep breaths, settle yourself, and get comfortable. After several minutes of relaxation, answer the following five questions:

1) When is the first time you felt utterly powerless in a situation? Describe your age, circumstance, and your thoughts and feelings at the time.

_____

_____

_____

Trauma and Transformation: A 12-Step Guide.

2) How were you hurt in that situation?

_____

_____

_____

_____

3) Can you see your true level of responsibility? (If you were a child, remember that **children are 100% innocent**, and do not have the inner tools and resources to respond in a logical, mature way. So however you reacted was perfect for you at the time. Maybe no one ever told you this).

_____

_____

_____

_____

4) From your perspective *now*, did you really have any power over the situation; to change it in ANY way?

5) If you did try to change the situation, what would have been, or what were, the consequences?

_____

_____

_____

_____

THE POWER IN POWERLESSNESS

Like Daniel and survivors in general, recovery is about searching for and utilizing your true power. Your *True Power* is your core inner being; some refer to as the Soul, Spirit, God, Higher Power, etc. The power of admitting powerlessness, when that is the case, is that you can now move your attention and focus on the areas you **do** have control over. This releases your energy that was once so bound and invested in controlling what you do not have control over. Although this is a frightening idea, it is also the first liberating step in the discovery journey towards your real source of strength, integrity, power and ultimately, to accepting all parts of yourself.

Abigail describes her experience with Step One as follows: *"As the eldest child to very strict and withholding parents, I learned that it is forbidden to have my needs met and to share my feelings,"* says Abigail. *"I felt terribly neglected on several levels as a child and I now learn how to look inside and ask myself, 'What do I really feel?' I started checking in with myself regularly to find out what my truth is and how I can fulfill my own needs."* This did not come easily for Abigail because she was very successful in her chosen profession, and simply didn't see the use of admitting she was powerless over anything. She certainly was not about to admit she powerless over a very painful upbringing. It happened decades ago, felt too agonizing and threatening, so why bother? Through working this step, and with the support of her therapist and support group, she gained the insight to see that she was powerless as a child and adolescent and her parent's behavior had nothing to do with her. This insight came with a river of tears, but her heart began to open. She started gaining strength in her adult life and was able not to lose control or a sense of personal power when someone withholds their approval or affection. *"Approval has always been an issue with me,"* says Abigail. *"So admitting that I'm powerless over the lack of approval and affection, I did not receive as a child, is the way for me to provide myself with the approval I am seeing outside of myself. I'm admitting that there's something in the past I did not have control over and that by trying to control the illusion, I kept myself enslaved to it. By trying to control the past and the present, I am going to lose even more than I already did as a child. What I am going to lose is my sanity, my peace of mind, my sense of stability. My reward continues to be being free from needing it. So it's well worth it."*

For Adam, Daniel, and Abigail, the focus is on regaining *true* personal power instead of thinking of themselves as powerless individuals. By looking inside and discovering the truth of one's limitations, you become truth-seekers, you gain an understanding of personal power, and learn to easily recognize situations where you are, and where you are not, in control. This will directly influence your ability to effectively manage your life and circumstances.

During my years of being in recovery, I witnessed some amazing transformations in people who have had the courage to face the truth in their stories. They start with Step

One because they do not find it acceptable to be depressed or riddled with fear, and they are not satisfied with merely coping either. *Trauma Survivors want to claim joy as a way of life:* they want to find the truth about themselves, the truth about the traumatic event(s) and express themselves with authenticity.

I have the blessing to be fortunate enough to see Trauma Survivors become much more active by searching out answers and finding solutions to their hurts and painful memories *that is real for them.* Being in recovery is exhilarating for me because I see firsthand the energy with which people are working on recovering from their particular pain. I see no "victim mentality" in their search for recovering memories and buried feelings, but an ongoing search for meaning, for working through what had previously been discarded, and to making a worthwhile contribution to life.

DENIAL AS THE LINCHPIN IN UNMANAGEABILITY

A word about *"unmanageability"*: If you magically found yourself on the other side of the door you've kept locked by your denial of what happened, and no longer need denial as a protective mechanism, what would you find, feel, and what would you create with your life? With this exercise, you can allow yourself the space and freedom to recognize your un-cleansed wound and understand how it causes you to suffer on some level. This also allows you, as a regular practice, to send your love and compassion to that wounded part of yourself; that part that struggled in silence for too long. By being responsive to it, in essence, you can turn the blood of the wound into gold. You live in a time of profound growth in the self – help movement. It is a time of significant change in the way we view and treat human suffering: that the human suffering of our time has a spiritual solution, and with every journey, it begins with the first step. If you are still asking yourself *"why rock the boat for something that happened long ago, that doesn't really bother me? Who needs that?!"* - You may gain some insight by answering these two questions:

1) What wound do I have that is festering in my unconscious, that I suspect may be holding me back in life?

_____

_____

_____

_____

2) Does this (answer in #1) contribute to some aspect of unmanageability and am I not living life to the fullest because of it? Is there any chance that the weight in my wound is comprised of unprocessed grief? Has this burden gotten too heavy for me?

_____

_____

THE ENERGY AND POWER OF STEP ONE

Although you may sometimes find it hard to believe, **healing is part of the laws of nature.** It is well established that healing the psyche directly influences healing of the body, and with Step One, there is a new possibility for healing from trauma. In the practice of "admitting" and therefore letting go of what you were NOT responsible for, Step One is the energy and power of FREEDOM. This freedom has three variables: 1) not being able to control, or regulate the environment, 2) not being able to control your emotional or physical responses, and 3) how it affected you spiritually. What connects these three aspects is both the *force* of what happened, and that you had no power over what was actually happening to you, or around you. Such acknowledgment frees you from the bond of inappropriate responsibility, guilt, and illusion of control. Ultimately, such an acknowledgment is the golden key that unchains you from core, toxic, shame that is a result of certain types of trauma.

  As I have previously mentioned, and will mention throughout this book, unprocessed trauma, especially those that ***turn into wounds,*** can wear you down. When that energy remains latent, so does your creative potential. You can harness the energy of this step to power your creativity and create a life beyond your wildest dreams. For some people, myself included, my "wildest dreams" is psychological and emotional freedom. Take a moment to define your concept of "a life beyond my wildest dreams". Focus on your mental and emotional states, as it pertains to overcoming roadblocks, achieving emotional milestones in recovery, and outgrowing unhealthy fears.

_____

_____

_____

_____

However wonderful this all sounds, it still begs the question: *Who wants to "admit" to anything unpleasant, let alone what was once so frightening, out of control, and deeply painful?* I certainly did not waltz into my stored memory vault and whistle as I opened the rusted locks. My own resistance to opening the door was a readiness to peer into the window of my injured self and see where the disruption was; what I would have been like had the injury not occurred. The healing of this step gave me great insight into the powerlessness of the experiences and the resiliency of the Spirit that has her home in all of you. When I peered inside, I saw that this Spirit was there before the wounding took place and remains there no matter what. I also saw that accessing this Spirit would be well worth the grief work and the emotional excavation in order to work through the depression, anxiety, loneliness, and "long dark night" of childhood.

The tricky part is whether or not you have the awareness that you have a psychic wound as a result of surviving trauma and if recovery is what you really want. I say tricky because it not only requires honesty and confronting denial, but facing the pain, loss and grief. The power of denial is a protective mechanism and will not easily be given up without a fight. In applying Step One you admit that the effects of trauma have created situations of powerlessness requiring you to ask questions. Perhaps you were told that you were "making it up", didn't have "proof" that abuse occurred, or your particular traumatic experiences were invalidated and misunderstood. If this applies to you, you have a lot of company. Almost no one waltzes into the recovery process with bells and whistles, fearless and full of joy. Of course you can put this book down right now, and not go there. However, if you are reading this book, perhaps there is a part of you that admits that something in your life is unmanageable (self-define), and you no longer just want to get by. Remember that no one will come tap you on the shoulder to tell you that you are suffering, and most suffering is silent and known only to the sufferer.

The following are five questions to help you unleash the energy when an admission of powerlessness is made:

1) Why do you hold on to thinking that you have power over someone or something?

_____

_____

_____

_____

2) I believe that I am truly powerful over

_____ (something you

doubt that this statement is true over). Explain.

_____

_____

_____

_____

3) If I drop this belief and feel the truth of being powerless over it, this would immediately flood me with:

_____

_____

_____

_____

4) What "hungry ghost" (anything I am terrified to face) of mine am I fearful would come marching out of the closet if I really admit that I am powerless of what happened?

_____

_____

_____

_____

5) What did I learn about myself from answering these questions?

_____

_____

_____

_____

Perhaps you are feeling some feelings of grief, sadness, and anger. These are common feelings when acknowledging that you once did not have any control over your circumstances. For every moment you are courageous enough to let yourself feel, and not numb yourself or react inappropriately, you are exchanging it for a gold coin: the gold of a moment's serenity and letting go. When you process and therefore "let go", you are rewarding yourself with serenity.

Go ahead and try it out! Ask yourself if you would be willing to trade a moment of holding on to dark energy, for a moment of lightness and self-forgiveness. Would the exchange be worth it? Remember the Buddhist saying that *"whatever you run after, will run from you, and whatever you run from, will chase you"*. Are you ready to cease the game of hide-and-seek with your traumatic memories? If yes, describe what memories you are "on the run from" and why. What would happen if you sat with your memories and the attending feelings?

_____

_____

_____

_____

Trauma-recovery involves the mind, body, and soul. (For the purpose of this book, the discussion will primarily revolve around the spiritual and psychological realm of the healing. There are many wonderful books on the subject of body healing and I encourage the interested reader to further explore the subject). Trauma Survivors, who have not worked through what happened, fight a battle within themselves to achieve self-esteem, and manage the fear and sadness that manifests in many different ways.

The real transformation in a Trauma Survivor happens when she is completely on her own side, discovers that although powerless at the time, she is no longer powerless now, discovers her true needs, and uses her ego in a healthy way for processing and transformation. This Survivor, who has reached this insight and relief from letting go of unnecessary burden, is ready to explore Step Two.

Samaya means not holding anything back, not preparing our escape route, not looking for alternatives, not thinking that there is ample time to do things later... It softens us so that we can't deceive ourselves. [3]

Pema Chodron

---

[3] Chodron, Pema. *When Things Fall Apart: Heart Advice for Difficult Times.* (Boston, MA: Shambhala Publications, Inc. Horticultural Hall, 1997), 164.

STEP TWO

Came to believe that a Power greater than ourselves could restore us to sanity.

When I first met Adam, it was not obvious why he came to me for help with the Twelve Steps. From a superficial look at his life he appeared to have every reason to be a trusting person. He described his successful love-relationship, healthy and smart children, a genuine love for his work, and a satisfying social life. His life would be the envy of most people, with a bank account, and external factors that most people dream of. Unlike many people who turn to the Twelve Steps because of addictive patterns of behavior in their lives, Adam turned to the Twelve Steps because a friend had urged him to seek help using spiritual principles that have helped countless others.

Over lunch, Adam confided in me: *"I don't understand why this Step feels so impossible to me, because I don't have any good reason to be so untrusting. God has always provided for me, and I think I have coped very well in life so far."* He described Step Two as his biggest hurdle, until I reminded him that *"...Came to..."* refers to a process, arriving from a place of being spiritually unconscious, to increased consciousness. His struggle with Step Two, along with other background information, indicated to me that perhaps there were frozen pockets of pain inside him. Asking him to *..."come to believe..."* was touching on this area. He admitted to being an expert at hiding and keeping the secrets of his childhood trauma, and how he never really believed that anything or anybody can help him. Step Two really challenged him. I asked him how he felt acknowledging this, and he whispered to me: *"I am really unhappy in my life, deep down; no matter what it looks like on the outside. Just being aware of this makes me feel so raw and vulnerable."*

Adam explained that his emotional life was not on firm ground. He felt a strong need to hide emotionally, and that he does not "trust a soul", let alone "a Power greater than himself." He struggled to admit that this concept was very unfamiliar to him, and "trust" was not a logical proposition for him. Although he expressed feeling profound relief in being able to "come clean" about his emotional life, and to see through his own denial, he felt terrified at the pain he felt when his frozen pockets of pain began to thaw. He experienced this thawing out as: *"facing my childhood secrets, and then getting permission to seek some kind of help. I don't really know about the rest of this spiritual solution stuff"*. Adam unwittingly described the essence of Step Two: **to arrive at a place where he can ask for help (spiritual principle of hope).**

Like many trauma survivors, Adam could appear to be strong and trusting. But often internally, there is a sense of being out of touch and unfamiliar with trusting what is safe and real. During our step work together, the reasons for Adam's lack of trust (and difficulty with this step) became clear. Adam was largely abandoned by his parents, who only took time to provide for his basic physical needs. His father was away most of the time for work, and when he was home, rarely made eye-contact with him. There was virtually no communication between them. Adam's mother remained in her room, with the lights out, most of the time, and when she interacted, would go into screaming fits of rage. As a small child, Adam had no opportunity to receive the loving encouragement, love, safety and stability that a child needs to develop trust. In his home environment, he had to fight hard for any bit of recognition. In his adult life he had to fight hard to trust that things would be okay. Beneath his perfectionist, over-achieving persona was man who felt weak, drained, and limited.

In his relationship, Adam hid his lack of trust, and his partner could not understand why Adam *"never fully let go and sees that I am safe"*. Adam grudgingly admits that he does not trust his partner or anyone, and has made a life for himself in spite of so little trust *in anyone.* But the lack of a trusting foundation internally was catching up to him. It seemed too painful to go on like this. *"Perhaps everyone in the world has someone to trust in, except for me"*, began Adam's nagging inner voice. No one teaches you trust and if you suffered a trauma, this sense of trust can be seriously undermined. Adam had the same questions that are typical for trauma survivors: *"*W*hy me!? If there is a God, how can God allow this to happen in its presence? How and why can I trust? I will only be lead to further disappointment, rejection, and suffering."*

Adam worked hard to ignore the growing feeling that he did not want to go on like this, but did not know how to change it. He had started to feel chronically guilty about his lack of trust and for weeks he would apologize to me whenever he admitted that he did not trust me or the step work we were doing together. His lack of basic trust was apparent in his disparagement of his fearful state of mind. However, what he learned over time is that the words *"Come to..."* in this step, suggests that people learn at different levels, and as long as Adam gave himself permission to trust the process, *"the Twelve Steps continue to be my personal roadmap out of hell. I now experience joy and acceptance, because I really get it that learning to trust is a process, and it's different for everyone. And the starting point is from whatever level of trust you have, or do not have. Life sends me things and my Higher Power is silently there for me. It's an entirely different approach to life".*

In social work we say: *"Start from where the client is".* This applies to trust issues: if you feel you cannot trust enough to ask for help, then you have just identified your starting point. You will begin your journey from the place of *"I don't / can't trust*". During his process of recovery from trauma by applying the Twelve Steps, Adam learned the difference between belief and trust. A person can believe that a spiritual power exists; but that does not mean that he necessarily trusts that power. It is now easier for Adam to trust that a power greater than himself can help him go from feeling deeply fragmented, to a restoration to wholeness (sanity).

MANY TRAUMA SURVIVORS ARE STRUGGLING

As I listen to others on the Twelve Step journey, I find myself searching for the main stumbling blocks in trust that trauma survivor's face. It is true that traumatic events shake up your world, have you questioning the meaning of life, and this puts up barriers to trust. The goal of trusting a power greater than you can be an exacting taskmaster. Healers, clinicians and fellow travelers have opened the way for you to enter the door of healing and transformation. They have extended the parameters of what you thought you were capable of. As a result, many survivors are attempting to do much more to heal than what once was just a longing. From listening to other survivors, I know that living life with unhealed wounds is unsatisfying and painful for a great many men and women. They find themselves living life on two different stages, and in two different theatres. On the outside, their lives look a certain way, yet internally they yearn for an emotional life that is free from suffering and loneliness.

Survivors, especially, often hide their fundamental lack of trust. Operating in a superficial world, fighting for respect, and lacking in support to pursue a spiritual life, survivors press ahead in spite of their collection of battle scars. Such people find themselves greatly challenged to maintain an appearance of having it all together, as they go through their professional and personal life. The challenge lies in working to express those parts of them that are unhealed, and are longing to trust and to be fully expressed, *without being seen as weak*. This applies equally to both men and women. Survivors are struggling with courage and determination to make their lives work, in spite of this great, gaping wound.

The survivor's struggle to trust in these two theaters is further complicated because each theater requires different, even oppositional, sets of skills. It is very stressful to maintain a certain front to the public, and then have to contend with that sense of disconnect and lack of trust, inwardly. Many survivors expect themselves to cope and be okay with these extremely different realities.

Applying Step Two to the struggle of healing this aspect of the traumatic wound (difficulty trusting, and difficulty with authority figures), begins with a careful inspection into the programming of a trauma survivor. Somewhere in a survivor's programming is a single operative principle, which at once holds the person back trying to heal and grow in this area, but keeps him putting up a front, perhaps even leading to relationships that do not work, dead-end jobs, or boring routines. In this area of trust, which Step Two directly addresses, the survivor is undeveloped. But most survivors I know are not lazy or uninterested in their growth. The people I interact with on my journey are living busy lives, focused on recovery and growth, even though they feel that trusting anything, or anyone - let alone an invisible power- is frightening, and impossible. Step Two can help you get unstuck and able to trust, where trust was once so frightening and impossible.

BETRAYAL, LOSS AND AUTHORITY FIGURES

My personal experience and professional work have led me to believe that the main thought pattern that gets in the way of a survivor's attempts at trusting a Safe Other, or Higher Power, is the fear that trust will lead to betrayal and loss. There is also the fear of authority figures, and also the desire to rebel against authority figures. Enormous losses have been sustained by trauma survivors, and often survivors have been abused by people in authority (including parents). However, these losses are often overlooked by the person who focuses only on the more dramatic components of trauma.

An adult survivor who appears on the outside to have it all together, but inwardly experiences a lack of trust for everything and everyone, may not experience relief upon disclosing this openly. She may instead be acutely aware of the loss of trust for her caregiver, society, or in life being good. And an individual, who has experienced the prolonged divorce of his parents, death of a sibling, or death of a parent, loses hope in a bright future. The survivor's loss of trust (whenever this occurred), together with a sense of betrayal, disturbs the very base of one's sense of security. If the traumatic incident occurred in childhood by a caregiver, the child has no choice but to translate that into "*I am unworthy. This happened to me because I am bad. The world is a bad, threatening place. I do not deserve better.*" If a child has been betrayed by her primary caregiver, and therefore cannot trust him or her, she will feel that no one in the world is safe to trust. When her energy is tied up with trying to build emotional fortresses or hiding from the world, she has little energy with which to grow emotionally, psychologically and spiritually.

When you apply Step Two to your own life, you can begin the process of developing a sense of trust for *safe others*. The essence of Step Two is coping with loss, including grieving for what is now gone and cannot be undone (perhaps you were once a very trusting person; innocent and vulnerable, and something or someone robbed that from you). It is also about learning to know a Power greater than yourself, as a loving, sustaining energy, and not as an authority figure that will harm or control you. Step Two is also about achieving some cognitive understanding that no matter what happened to you, a Power greater *than yourself **can** restore you to sanity and integrity*. Think about this for a moment. You are not to be blamed for your loss of trust, or any other reaction or formed beliefs. Actually, it was a perfect response in the context of what happened.

As part of taking Step Two, feel free to express your anger and pain at having experienced such a profound loss of trust in the past. Once you have appropriately and sufficiently expressed your anger and pain, you have cleared the way for the possibility in trusting that a Power greater than yourself is: a) greater than your wounds, and b) has the **capability** to help in your healing **no matter what you suffered**. (If you are too angry at God and blame God for your experiences, you are proving that you do, in fact, believe in a God. And at this point, your understanding of God is one of inflicting pain and / or standing by coldly as you suffered. As you journey through the Twelve Steps with an open mind, you may discover new information about the role of **self-will** versus **God's will**, and how this has had tragic implications for humanity. You may also discover that numerous sufferers confuse these two, and can take this misunderstanding with them to the grave, acting it out in life to their detriment. I hope you will not be one of them.

The process of overcoming the trauma and utilizing the power and energy of Step Two is not an easy one for most survivors. The Ego, (your internal psychological system that meets your needs and solves your problems), will step in and protest: *"Trust is not safe! I cannot believe in anyone! Whom can I really trust!?"* This is where you become painfully aware that you lack trust, and find yourself suspicious of life, in general, and of people. After all, you have numerous examples of life appearing as painfully unpredictable and at times, unfair.

Since the dawn of time people have been searching to answer the question of why there is human suffering, and more specifically, where is God when these bad things happen? This is an even more burning question for survivors with very real and unanswered questions as to why they should trust. It is typical for survivors to be well-defended against the pain, as this defense at the core, is self-protection. Naturally, you want to prevent yourself from being hurt again. This desire is especially urgent when you feel life cheated you or when you have been betrayed by other people, *let alone if caregivers were the perpetrators*. The tragic side to this self-protection is that by trying to protect yourself from further harm, you feed an illusion of control.

When you go about your life this way, you are left with a life that is more difficult and empty because you have a deep sense of isolation. **Mistrust takes away the very search for meaning. You need someone or something in life that you can believe in, trust in, and rely upon.**

When a survivor faces Step Two with hope that he will be able to "come to believe", he puts aside his long-held illusion of control. He begins to have an opening of the heart. I define the opening of my heart as **grand healing through the redemptive love of compassion.** The grand healing that occurred for me in this step was opening a place in my heart, however small, that allowed for the possibility of a guiding Presence, more loving than all the loving people I ever encountered, wiser than all the wise people I admired, and more compassionate than I was able to imagine. I very slowly began to let this Presence in.

Early in my recovery, a woman with decades of recovery told me during a mid-night conversation: *"Rivka, you can borrow my Higher Power, until you find your own."* She said this in response to my telling her that I had no concept of a loving Higher Power, or what it means to be *"restored to sanity."* Years later I called her up and thanked her for her loving Higher Power that she lent me; I am returning it now because I had found my own. And I genuinely did. I *"came to believe"* over the years that a power greater than myself whom I choose to call *"My Creator"*, is powerful and loving enough to restore me to sanity (integrity and connectedness to true self).

When your psyche is ready to believe in "a power greater than yourself" you recognize that you are not alone, although you felt very alone during the traumatic events. You no longer go through life with an inward, secret struggle trying do everything all by yourself. With Step Two, you start the *incredibly powerful and beneficial process* of letting go of illusions that take you down very painful roads. Step Two is a gradual process towards developing trust in all that is good and whole, to experience life with a bit more ease and perhaps even some joy.

In taking Step Two, you accept five golden keys to the healing of trauma. The **first key** is that when you admit that you do not trust, you are on the path to claiming that trust back. The **second key** is in your personal understanding of the dynamics of surviving traumatic losses or betrayal (what does this mean for you personally, how has it affected you, etc). The **third key** is that you begin your process of overcoming *the fear* of trusting. The **fourth key** is overcoming the need to be isolated and in hiding, and to learn who and what is safe and reliable to trust. And the **fifth key** is the understanding of how you would like to be living your life, with a sense of trust in a power greater than yourself. With these **five golden keys**, you will discover untapped energies and hidden talents. This is my understanding of being restored to "sanity", guided by the True Self.

My personal beginnings of finding someone or something to believe in began with the power of the kindness I witnessed in other people. As I became more and more receptive to other's kindness, I replaced my old projection of God as distant, unloving, punishing and cold – with the understanding that God has qualities of warmth, kindness and acceptance. I had a changed perspective as a result of being willing to trust the right people.

However, this is a very personal process and it is different for each individual. The knowledge that what you believe in is *your personal choice* is a great start on the Twelve Step path, because, as survivors, you have lived through conditions that perhaps lead to an impairment of trust whatsoever. Utilizing your free choice, you can choose to further explore the truth about a matter, even a subject as complex as "why do bad things happen to good people". Survivors also struggle with trusting their own inner guidance because you once had to sacrifice this knowledge and silence this voice in order to remain out of harm's way.

In my work with survivors, I have observed the following emotional conditions that have their origins in traumatic experiences. Such conditions will pose as a great challenge for the survivor wanting to take Step Two:

- Belief that I am to blame for what happened, so why would anyone do anything good for me like "restore me to sanity"? (I am undeserving.)
- Belief that I am as powerless as I was when traumatized (so how will trust help if I am powerless and I cannot 'see' this Being?)

- Loss and betrayal is doomed to be repeated, so why try? I don't need the heartache! (Anticipation that all relationships will ultimately end up in disappointment.)
- Having a sense of deep shame and alienation from others because of my experiences, which *no one* can *ever* find out about! (I am doomed to be shamed and rejected.)
- Acting on destructive tendencies which may include addictive behaviors and other destructive coping mechanisms. (If I am bad, which I must be since no one rescued me, who cares what I do to myself?)
- Attachment and/or sexual disorders (a genuine block to experiencing long-lasting trust and intimacy).
- Abandoning myself to support, please, placate, or rebel against others; instead of being firmly on my own side.

A survivor must deal with the silent tears waiting to be cried, and that he may not totally be understood or accepted when he begins his process. He may realize that those around him are not going to support him and they may not be trustworthy. He may have to seek outside sources of support and develop a healthy network so he can take the necessary steps to self-forgiveness and self-trust.

"I WILL BE THAT WHICH I WILL BE" (Exodus 3:14)

In the Hebrew Bible, when Moses asked God to tell him whom he shall say sent him, God replied that Moses should use the name: *"Ehyeh asher ehyeh"* (Exodus 3:14). This phrase has several possible English translations: *"I Am that I Am"*, r *"I will be"*, *"I will be that which I will be"* or *"I shall be"*. The Hebrew word *"Hayah"* means "*existed*" or "*was*"; and the word "*ehyeh*" is translated *"I will be"*. I had a spiritual awakening when I carefully read this verse and tried to apply it to my life. **I saw this phrase as the best proof and explanation for Step Two.** These simple words contain the most welcoming invitation and direction **for all people.** It is well-known that throughout human history, (and surely for those who are not yet on this earth), that most of humanity have never agreed on one single understanding or name of God. This verse implies the great news that God already factored in for this, understanding that this is part of humanity's course, and is not limited by how human's reference this Deity.

The hope in Step Two begins a restorative process of internal connection and attachment, which is possible even if your early childhood attachments were severed, chaotic, or non-existent. In working on repairing a sense of connection, it might be helpful to get to know the Power behind the Name by asking "*__who is the Seeker in me__*?" Perhaps your understanding of God is that something within you that moves you through life. For some survivors, it is their experiences in life that have been stronger than their personal beliefs. Since you are limited as a human being, it is not necessary to fully understand this Force of Life, but rather to accept, or surrender, to this Mystery. The good news is that the *"Power greater than ourselves"* is a constant, loving presence, whether or not you feel you deserve it, understand this Power, love this Power in return, feel it, accept it, or can explain it. It always exists as a safe, gentle, and unconditional love, demanding nothing in return. According to Kabala (Jewish mysticism), God chooses to be right here with your human experience, to experience with you your suffering, tragedy, joy, and everything in between. These are the attributes of a highly personal and compassionate Creator, who desires closeness with Its creation.

Take a few minutes now to ponder the meaning of this in your life, and write your thoughts and feelings below.

_____

_____

_____

_____

Every survivor comes to connect with, and believe in a Higher Power, in their own way and time. The key is to set aside the self-judgment, and/or *other people's opinions* that belief in a Higher Power must look a certain way. If God is not personal to you, you will not experience the personal love that this relationship affords. The love is always there, but you will not be receptive to it.

EXERCISE TO CONNECT WITH A HIGHER POWER

Draw two lists. On the first list, put down every characteristic that your dream Higher Power does **not** have. On the second list, put down all the characteristics that your dream Higher Power **does** have. Allow yourself to be creative, bold, courageous, open-minded, and truly reflective of what you dream for in this ultimate connection. When you are finished, see if you notice any patterns. For example, you may notice that with each quality you listed in the "not have" column, you were once hurt in this way. Perhaps you are still being hurt by such qualities, either from yourself or from someone else. In the "does have" column, you may notice that you are deeply touched by these qualities, either by having them yourself, or through other people.

Trauma and Transformation: A 12-Step Guide.

CHARACTERISTICS THAT MY DREAM HP DOES NOT HAVE:	CHARACTERISTICS THAT MY DREAM HP DOES HAVE:

When I did this exercise, I immediately noticed that the list of who my Higher Power was NOT, had all the characteristics of the people that took advantage of me, and mistreated me. I was blocked from having a sense of a loving higher power until I did this exercise, because I did not realize that unconsciously I had only one image of God, and it was a very negative, unloving, and limited image. (The clinical term for an internal image is "schema".) Step Two afforded me the gift of bringing this information to the light of my consciousness. I realized that this untrue, negative image of God did not have to be the case for the rest of my life.

When I viewed my second list of the characteristics of my "dream Higher Power", a new and permanent concept began to form, which was unlike my old, archaic one. I felt a new sense of hope, and view of life. I saw a lot of my own qualities, and I realized that if I believed in my own basic goodness, certainly, I could believe in a Higher Power with whom I shared some qualities! At the very least, I began to believe that I am basically a good, compassionate, empathic, and conscientious person.

From this new starting point, I became willing to trust in a Higher Power that is incomprehensibly many times each of these positive qualities, and none of the negative qualities. I adopted, and attached myself, to this new schema of God. Internalizing this updated schema gave me much deeper access to my gifts, my own heart, and ultimately to a more accurate understanding of a Higher Power. I no longer thought of God as something outside of me, with little connection or genuine interest in me. For some people, relying on a masculine image of a paternal, reward-and-punishment God is a comfortable fit, but for me, this is no longer the case. I connect with the "*Shechina*" (pronounced in Hebrew as the she-cheenah, which is the divine feminine), or a neutral image of strong, silent, and loving presence.

There are many other images of a personal God, and the practice of creating your personal idea of a guiding spirit, is the foundation for this step. Step Two does not say, "We came to believe *in* a Power greater than ourselves.", but rather **that** a Power greater than ourselves **could** restore us to sanity." There is no emphasis on what or who this Power is; only on what this Power can do for you, which is restoring you to "sanity". Step Two is also about seeking the power within yourself, which I personally understand as my Divine Soul. I connect to my Soul through my True Self, and through this unity, I connect with my Higher Power. In fact, the whole process of the Twelve Steps is a journey to my True Self, because without this relationship, I cannot genuinely connect to my soul, to my higher power, or to anyone else.

Developing a sense of self has been a critical component to my healing, and I discovered, to my delight, that there really is a power in me that is far greater than the small self I thought I was. It is my True Self, that was layered beneath a False Self, I thought was the real me. I am now living in harmony with my True Self and I got in the habit of turning to it for guidance in all my affairs. I fully cooperate with it because it is that part of me that carries truth and wisdom. This relationship has brought me into balance and harmony with myself. My primary spiritual practice is seeking, and cooperating with this Source of Wisdom and Creativity. It is a great way to go through life! It is only from this state of consciousness that I am able to love myself and others. This is how I live Step Two.

WHAT'S "SANITY" AND "INSANITY" GOT TO DO WITH IT?

For survivors of trauma, you may be puzzled by this step's implication that you had been insane. It seems like an awfully huge leap from acknowledging your powerlessness over traumatic experiences, to admitting your "insanity".

Trauma and Transformation: A 12-Step Guide.

Now is the time to take a good look at what the concept of "insanity" means. Answer the following six questions.

1. Did I believe I could control the traumatic event? What were some of my attempts at this, and what were the results of my efforts?

   _____

   _____

   _____

   _____

2. What things were done to me that I had no control over, and that I believe I was guilty for?

   _____

   _____

   _____

   _____

3. Did I put myself in dangerous situations to deny, forget, or erase what happened?

___

4. Do I believe that I am responsible and "deserve" what happened? How has this belief played out in my life?

___

5. Did I make insane decisions as a result of the emotional wounding, the hurt, the pain and the fear?

___

6. Did I ever physically, sexually or psychological injure myself or anyone else as a result of my unprocessed trauma?

For trauma survivors *insanity* is a loss of your perspective and your sense of proportion. **It is safer to believe that something is wrong with you than to be aware of the painful reality of what happened.** This is especially true for survivors who have been victims of sexual, physical, psychological, or emotional abuse, either as children, adolescents or adults. *It is often safer and easier to believe* *you were the crazy one, than to remember how you once were hopeless and abandoned in an abusive situation.* If your experiences happened a long time ago, or the abuse was subtle, you may discover that a whole new level of denial is making it hard to see the insanity in your life. You may need to become familiar with the ways in which you have been insane in order to start caring about the hurt you are carrying around with you. Do not hold back about admitting that you believe you are responsible for the trauma you experienced. This guilt is "insane" on some level.

In our culture we accept the definition of "insane" as the loss of mind, the loss of ability to differentiate between right and wrong, or just plain crazy. But the term "insanity" can be applied to a survivor who goes through life with the unhealthy, erroneous belief that she is the guilty party for events that were out of her control. This belief creates a chain reaction of other unhealthy behaviors, and it is therefore imperative that the survivor seeking relief begin with an exploration of this.

When a survivor learns to combine the strength from a belief in a Higher Power and apply it to the insanity of false beliefs and a pain-based schema, she discovers the unique power of spiritual energy. If you lack sensitivity to safe spiritual energy, opening the doors to your traumatic experience can make you vulnerable. I encourage you to expand your definition and experience of "safe spiritual energy" to include art, beautiful music, nature, or anything that is gentle, open, and truthful. As the hurt part of you grows and heals, you will fulfill your function of meeting your needs in a healthy way, and you will shed your false, pain-based beliefs, thoughts and feelings.

Alternatively, by not using spiritual energy, you are settling for a life that is unnecessarily difficult and often painful and lonely, **regardless of what mask you wear.** You will suffer with problems that stem from the hurt parts of you, instead of solving them. You will have a tendency to wallow in negative feelings unnecessarily. But when you use your Higher Power, you will be provided, *externally and internally*, with the necessary support to heal the negative experiences and maintain good feelings. Without a spiritual foundation to recover from traumatic wounds, you may not have the knowledge or ability to establish appropriate boundaries. You may even be living your life expressed through a personality that is false, approval-driven, and under the control of the culture and family that programmed you. The anger, resentment and hurt you feel at living out this "insanity" will find expression inappropriately – toward loved ones, yourself, and those around you. If you do not have a genuine, *personal* concept of a loving Spirit, you may have the tendency to feel either like a victim of bad luck or a recipient of occasional good luck. If you have ***true*** beliefs about yourself, you are in charge of your life and make good things happen for yourself. **Do not be concerned with theological elegance or doctrinal adherence – just find a Power greater than yourself that works for you and makes sense. This power need only be perfectly loving and greater than your suffering.**

REVIEW AND MOVING ON

Before you move on to Step Three take some time to do the following exercise. Write out three columns. The title of the **first** column is: *"All the areas that I am not willing to, or have not yet, given to God".* The title of the **second** column is: *"What I am afraid of if I give these things over to God?"* The title of the **third** column is: *"What God wants me to be"* (opposite experience of why I am not willing to give certain areas over) when I feel my fears (associated with what I won't give over).

STEP TWO EXERCISE IN COMING TO BELIEVE

All the areas that I am not willing to, or have not yet, given to God.	What I am afraid of if I give these things over to God?	What God wants me to be?

After you have done this, answer the following three questions, in order to assess how you have internalized the spiritual principles underlying Step Two.

1. What is my understanding of this step?

   _____

   _____

   _____

   _____

2. What am I doing to overcome any unrealistic, false, or otherwise erroneous beliefs that I may be harboring about the trauma I experienced?

   _____

   _____

   _____

   _____

3. Am I at peace with not yet believing, but being *willing* to believe in this power? Do I trust that if I walk in the direction of a personal faith, I will eventually find it?

_____

_____

_____

_____

In your traumatic experiences, you may have been alone, in extreme pain and isolated. Now you have an opportunity to be released from the blind pursuit of your illusions, false beliefs and unnecessary suffering. You no longer have to struggle to keep your traumatic experiences a secret or isolate yourself to hide your pain. You can experience belonging by seeing that you are part of a larger universe that supports, nurtures and values you. With the support of this foundation and newfound faith, you can achieve the willingness and trust to participate in the transformative work of your recovery.

YOU ARE INVINCIBLE

*Let me walk
with my own self
in a wondrous, glorious dream.
And down this path
that we shall tread,
we'll be an invincible team.* [4]

---

[4] Dooley, Mike. *Choose Them Wisely Thoughts Become Things!* (Hillsboro, Oregon: Atria Books/Beyond Words Publishing, Inc., 2009), 51.

STEP THREE

Made a decision to turn our will and our lives over to the care of God as we understood Him.

You have worked Steps One and Two with a safe and trusted person – you have surrendered and you have demonstrated your willingness to try a new approach to your life experiences. When you admit your powerlessness over your traumatic history, you learn a comforting and critical truth: that you experienced certain painful life events that you absolutely could not have controlled. You were also not always in control of the coping patterns that have emerged. For some survivors, this can be a frightening and humbling experience. (More of this will be revealed through the Fourth and Fifth Steps).

In addition to your traumatic life experiences, there are numerous things in life you cannot control. Your willingness to view your experiences in a different light infuses you with a new sense of hope and relief. However, if you do not translate your hope into action, you will revert to old behaviors. Your old behaviors, formulated by you as coping mechanisms, leave you feeling resentful, frustrated and angry. As a trauma survivor, you try to be in control in many different ways. Using your sexuality as punishment or reward, using guilt, dishonesty or "learned helplessness" to get your way, you try to get the results you want. Another very common dysfunctional behavioral approach in dealing with people is trying to "take care of" or "fix" things, even if it is unsolicited, unnecessary or inappropriate. Some of you may resort to threatening others, manipulating, or bullying to get your way, even if these tactics are not necessarily used maliciously.

Beneath the desire to influence a situation to go your way, is your frantic efforts to avoid feeling the fear, anxiety and powerlessness that is already there. It can challenge you to be in a situation where you are triggered into feeling that you are submitting to someone's demands or that you are being taken in a direction that you do not consciously choose to go.

When you find yourself caught in the endless loop of such a power struggle, you carry an emotional burden that is unnecessary and heavy. **All of your psyche's energy goes into keeping you from falling from the staggering weight, instead of investigating the cause for this maladaptive behavioral pattern, and rectifying it.** Until you <u>make a decision, the central action in Step Three</u>, you cannot do anything about this burden you are struggling to remain in balance with. By making a decision, you are giving yourself permission to let go of your personal burdens. When you make a decision to put down your burden, you let go, allowing the space and energy for a creative and new life-force to take over.

However, trauma survivors may not find this idea easy or comforting, and the idea of making that decision may awaken a great terror in you. You can find a clue into why you have this fear, by pulling back the curtain and examining your inner stage for your schema of object constancy. This refers to the inner blueprint of your earliest childhood attachments. This is especially true when you examine what decision you are choosing to do here.

Perhaps making any decision is not something you have done in a long while, and are used to having decisions made for you by other people or circumstances. Maybe you were too frightened to make your own decisions, and life seemed simpler when you passively and without questioning, allowed others to drive the ship (excessive compliance). In addition, when you insert the idea of putting your will and life to the care of some Power you may not understand, or may still be frightened of (typical for survivors), you may just want to walk away or find another way to deal with the traumatic wound (distrust and suspiciousness). These thoughts are perfectly human, as the Third Step decision for some people, can be too big to make in one leap.

You can break this step down into a series of separate, smaller steps. The Third Step is just one component of the path of recovery from your traumatic wound. Unlike the common misunderstanding that making the Third Step decision means you must immediately and thoroughly change everything about the way you live, you allow the change to happen slowly and gradually. And most importantly, *you can let go of the fear that if you make the decision that this step calls for, you will be doing something that you are not ready for or will not like.*

It is especially important for survivors to take notice that the Third Step suggests you turn your will and your life over to the *care of* the God of *your* understanding. These words are significant because they mean that you are allowing someone or something **not to control you,** which you may be especially sensitive to, **but to care for you.** Perhaps you have not had any healthy experience of being cared for, because "care" meant control, conditions, suffocation, or manipulative intentions. Out of fear of the unknown and once having had their trust abused, most survivors will not welcome the idea of "letting go". You may misunderstand Step Three to mean that if you keep holding on, you will prevent more pain, and that letting go leaves open the unanswered question of who or what exactly will take charge?

By gaining insight into the way you need to control and how your fear of letting go was influenced by the traumatic experiences, you will develop an awareness of your personal stumbling blocks and inhibitions. **In your decision-making,**

you let go of *your attachment to what you want* (self-will), and replace it with the care of a power greater than yourself, as you understand this Power. This decision will provide you with direction for the growth of your own spiritual evolution. For you to be able to profit from Step Three, you must have a concept of what a decision is, and then commit yourself to following principles of spiritual growth. The **first** critical principle of spiritual growth is to keep an open mind. The **second** critical principle is that the more you derive your sense of self externally, the more you live in fear and dependency. *<u>Survivors will often describe their sense of self as unpredictable and fragmented. This motivates them to seek a "self" outside of themselves</u>*.

The reason that keeping an open mind is so important is because it will allow you to examine the adaptations you have made in relation to others. This causes you to become fearful to being cared for in a healthy way (due to personal boundary problems, suspiciousness, and distrust). Many survivors have a part of themselves that is completely closed off to receiving healthy care and love, and therefore they cannot conceive of making the decision required in this step. This is typical for survivors who have suffered impairment in the area of attachment. You must be honest about your own experiences and how they have affected you.

A common barrier for trauma survivors with Step Three is that you may have gotten very used to creating barriers to receiving care from others. This is not the case for everyone, but for many this is true. The painful dynamics between you and the people who abused you, created the distance that you feel towards a possible caring presence. You cannot work on honestly making the decision to turn your will and care over to a higher power, unless you are committed to the reality principle: *seeing the situations you went through and the people involved for what they really are.* Perhaps your trauma experience was chronic rejection and abuse at home; and you never felt cared for. If that happened to you, Step Three may seem impossible because the idea of "truly cared for" triggers in you the emotional states of confusion, anxiety, fear, feelings of disconnect or withdrawal. The challenge is to keep an open mind, allowing for the *possibility* that you will be able to feel, experience, and receive the care of your Higher Power. The opposite of an open mind is *denial* (pretending something does not exist), and that will keep you stuck. It may be helpful to review your answers in Step One, to compare your level of openness and acceptance at this point.

DENIAL'S OPPOSITES: TRUTH AND AWARENESS

If you are capable of being honest, you will find that you will be able to affirm the decision required in Step Three, because surrender to the truth breeds awareness. In the presence of truth and awareness, you can create an internal environment which will provide you with the option to receive your Higher Power. The welcome sign outside your door can have any name that you please – the important thing is that you first create an internal space, followed by a genuine invitation! This third step decision is an invitation. It is also an affirmation that although you once thought of yourself as guilty, or maybe even unworthy of this "care", that such a disturbance in self-concept was a false belief and a fraudulent compromise. You put out an invitation to the God of your understanding by saying the words of Step Three out loud, or in any way that expresses your understanding of what this step means for *you*. If you choose to pray as your way of taking Step Three, bear in mind that the difference with "*praying a prayer*" (a commitment), is not the same thing as *saying a prayer* (which can often be obligatory, rote, institutionalized and impersonal).

In my own experience, I found that the commitment of Step Three includes becoming willing to look for solutions of recovery that work for me. Your personal turning point is in choosing to go from identifying as a victim of what happened in life, to *seeking solutions that work for change.* This begins by being honest about your particular needs, and affirming that every person needs to be cared for, *including you.* Survivors may feel challenged when it comes to admitting their need for care and love (because of internalized shame, guilt, fear and inaccurate self-esteem). **However, once you allow for God's care in your life, you will see how your receptivity to this care will empower you. It is truly a spiritual breath of fresh air! I believe that God's will for every person is for love, joy, and abundance.**

Some survivors find it helpful to practice Step Three in their lives by remembering that if something is anything other than Love, it is not God's will, but self-will. **When you 'self-**

will' your way through life, even if you think you have 'made a decision', you are practicing 'hook-backs', which means that after you let something go, you did not unhook it; you intentionally left the hook in there, so you can take it back at any point. Everything you receive in life is by the Grace of a Higher Power, and if you attempt to do **God's will all the time**, your life will make a lot of sense.

If you acknowledge your need to feel cared for, you are beginning the process of coming out of isolation. When you are going through life feeling cared for, you will feel strengthened by such an alliance. This new beginning, however, requires you to take an emotional risk of feeling cared for by a power greater than yourself. For many survivors, feelings of healthy caring, based in trust and truth, are unknown. To build on the first two steps, you must be willing to let go of any familiar feelings of need for chronic isolation and control. Instead, you must choose to take the risk of allowing yourself the experience of being cared for. This experience will follow your decision, which you can re-affirm as often as you need to.

This is easier said than done, and some of the main issues for trauma survivors will revolve around the meaning of cooperating with a loving higher power, and "turning your will over." For me, "turning it over" means to lessen my clenched grip on something, someone, an idea or an expectation. My ego, like those of most people, tries to convince me to cling to self-will, and old, comfortable habits that no longer serve me. I define "self-will", as an attachment to the idea that things must *always* go my way. However, survivors must take caution when defining willfulness because your will may have been broken in destructive ways (childhood abuse and trauma), and clarity of definition will go a long way in working this step.

The self-will you are committing to turning over here is the willfulness that leads to destructive acts. This is what I am seeking to replace with God's will. If I am always seeking to replace my willfulness with that of GOD (**G**ood **O**rderly **D**irection), I will benefit in ways that will create the ultimate security and peace inside of me. I am more than willing to exchange my FEAR (**F**rustration, **E**xpectations, **A**nxiety, **R**estless) with FAITH (**F**reedom, **A**cceptance, **I**nspired, **T**ouched, **H**eld).

Some of my personal benefits of Step Three, are that I developed strength in going through life without the incessant need to control, replacing old programming that no longer serves me (self-will), and to experience vitality, rigor, confidence and trust in a bright future. I also became conscious of when I was being driven to act in an unproductive way (self-will), as compared to making conscious choices (Good Orderly Direction/GOD).

Personal experience is far more powerful than a belief system, and when those two do not match, you can dismantle and dissolve the hooks that keep dysfunctional beliefs alive and well inside you. **This is the key to transformation**. If your personal issue that you struggle with, is not believing that you are cared for by your Higher Power, (a potent emotional issue), applying Step Three sincerely to your life, will help to loosen the compelling hold that this issue has on your life. It will be as if a spell has been broken, and this potent emotional reality that you have up until now, will lose force and fall away. Tragically, many survivors live their lives dictated by emotional schemas that are in fact no longer true in present-day reality, but the role of unprocessed shame and guilt. The reality is that your personal Creator cares for you, and you only need to be conscious of this, in order to experience it. It is that simple.

UNLOCKING YOUR NEED TO BE CARED FOR

When you start to doubt that you are worth caring for, say the third step out loud, as many times as you need to (try looking at yourself in the mirror while doing so). Pay attention to your thoughts, feelings, and bodily sensations. After you do this often enough, you will notice that there will be a sharp mismatch between your experience, and your old beliefs about being cared for. In that very moment of mismatch, providing you are disciplined enough not to fall back to old beliefs, you unlock yourself from a faulty belief. It is comparable to unlatching train cars that are connected to each other. This will allow you to create a life that is based on being cared for by God, instead of being controlled by long-ruling emotional realities that are not true or useful. It is not useful to go through life feeling that you cannot put yourself in the care of a Higher Power, or that you do not "deserve" this care. This care is your birthright; it is a natural response for your Creator to care for you, and such care is ever-present. If you are having a hard time with this concept, I suggest you explore what your emotional truth is that compels you to defend against this concept, despite the suffering that holding on to this idea causes for you. If you can retrieve from your unconscious what your emotional truth is around the issue of being cared for, I suggest you feel it emotionally, and then express it into words.

My friend in recovery, Melanie, told me in her own words, how she worked with Step Three: *"I started out adamantly believing that I've GOT to keep people's care and love out of my life, because if I allow someone to care for me it brings the betrayal and pain that killed my spirit as a child. I HAVE TO prevent that from happening to me. My parents were not communicative, except in an abusive way. That was the only 'caring' I ever received, until I became open-minded enough that perhaps a different kind of 'care' exists and is available for me".* Melanie retrieved her original pain around being in the care of abusive parents, and was vividly in touch with her pain and sadness around this. However, working on Step Three, put her also in touch with a completely opposite living knowledge that also felt perfectly true for her, but completely contradicted her original experience with being in the care of someone. Since both of these beliefs are so incompatible, yet very compelling, she felt anxiety, fear and doubt, **which is a common reaction when letting go of old ideas.** It is also a common response to repairing your concept of healthy relational engagement. **This is one core component of trauma recovery.**

Melanie and I continued to work together on Step Three until she was able to feel some vibrant personal truth that *intensely contradicted* her life-long and profound knowledge that being in the care of her Higher Power, would be pain-producing and detrimental to her spirit. She began journaling daily, specifically commenting on events that occurred in her daily living that was contradictory to her old belief (caring means pain and betrayal; the opposite reality of being cared for by a Higher Power). She wrote about her activities of daily living that are made possible because of her excellent health. This makes her feel really cared for by her Higher Power, and she wrote about it at the end of every day. I said to her, during one of our sessions, to picture and feel, as much as you can, how your physical health is one way that your Higher Power cares for you. Keep this image and feelings, as you add the other images and feelings of being your parent's child, and how neglected and betrayed you felt back then. *"Both images feel so true to me"*, Melanie replied. I told her that because they both felt so true for her, the ingrained and anxiety-provoking meaning of being cared for would be rendered null and void as an emotional reality. I explained that because she chose to try something new (Step Three), instead of her usual actions denying herself the experience of being cared for, her old system belief around this subject withered and fell away, losing all of its force.

Now when Melanie notices herself reverting to her old thoughts, she reads aloud her Third Step reminder: *"Come again??!! It is possible to be in the loving care of my Higher Power **and** remain deeply satisfied and pain-free!? The assumptions to the contrary have shaped my whole life, but are in fact false?"* She chose this particular wording because she found that **it respects her distress around the issue and helps her keep the awareness of both realities, which are in sharp contradiction to each other.** This allowed her to access her truth, and by not invalidating it, she would genuinely grow past it, and not merely suppress it. She was seeking a genuine transformational change in this area, and knew that if she would try to counteract her belief (*"care brings pain and betrayal"*), she would be using her own power to *force* a change.

However, by triggering this combination, she was using her inner power to change her personal reality. Melanie describes this as: *"I simply cooperate with and trust the Spirit that is inside of me. After a while of practicing and reminding myself of Step Three, this fear that was once a nameless, chokehold of a paralyzing power, was suddenly just not that much of a big deal. Now I can't imagine being cared for by my Higher Power as scary or full of pain and betrayal. That idea seems really silly to imagine"*. Like Melanie, and other survivors who have applied Step Three to their lives, **you can experience the same transformation.**

Say out loud the following, which I formulated as part of my own process in unlocking my need to be cared for by my loving Higher Power:

"Being cared for by my Higher Power is what I have decided upon as my source of love, power, and direction, long term."

Pay attention to how it feels in your body as you say this statement, at least 5 times, and then write your reactions below. Notice what emotions surface. With time and patience, a potent emotional theme, for example: "*It frightens me to be cared for*", may disappear.

_____

_____

_____

_____

Your *willingness* to receive the care of a power greater than yourself will produce a life-changing transformational shift, because it opens you to new, broader possibilities. You participate rather than trying to control life. There is enormous growth in this **if** you are willing and courageous enough to try a new approach and to let go of previous ways of doing things. All you need to do at this point is to take that first baby step, and a series of small baby steps following that first step. No one gets anything right without an appropriate amount of practice and patience, and this step is no different. If you are anything like the average person, you will find that your openness will come and go. However, as long as you remain on your personal spiritual path, a little bit of faith is enough to bring you back. When you feel like giving up, remember that you are wired for growth and change (neo-plasticity). By remaining honest, open and willing (H.O.W), you will be in the best position to change any negative and false beliefs about your Higher Power, yourself, and other people.

WRAP UP QUESTIONS

1) What do you think God's will is for you?

_____

_____

Trauma and Transformation: A 12-Step Guide.

_____

_____

2) Do you have a need for God's love in your life?

_____

_____

_____

_____

3) Is it apparent to other people that God's love is affecting your life?

_____

_____

_____

_____

4) What will it look like in your life, if you were only doing God's will?

_____

_____

_____

_____

5) What is your arch to personal freedom? (What is blocking you, and how will turning yourself over to God's care help to free you?)

_____

_____

_____

_____

6) What reaction do you have to the statement: *"There is no free-will; only self-will or God's will"*?

_____

_____

_____

_____

7) Do you think you know better than God?

_____

_____

_____

_____

8) How are you playing God in your life *right now*?

_____

_____

_____

_____

The purpose of answering these questions (and all the questions throughout this book) is to put you in touch with your Spirit. Being in touch with your spirit can assist you in having a personal experience with being cared for by a power greater than yourself.

> *"Someday our souls will be one and our union will be forever. I know that everything I give you comes back to me. So I give you my life, hoping that you will come back to me."* -Rumi

STEP FOUR

Made a searching and fearless moral inventory of ourselves.

Most survivors, unless they are in a crisis, do not put much thought into what happened; the people, places, things, and reactions to events that have long-shaped their life. But if you have not yet taken a look at what traumata shaped your personality, behaviors, fears, and ways of responding in life, Step Four is a good opportunity to stop and think about it. Perhaps you have reached the day when you realize that you are not living your life as you really want to. Perhaps you feel a deep inner longing for healthy, secure attachment, love and a more kind relationship with yourself. You may experience a longing for life as you were told it was supposed to be but you have no evidence that you are living such a life.

Step Four is the key to your *future* because it will help you see beyond what you think you know about yourself. Step Four will also help you to have conscious awareness of your personal reality, or personal filter system. This conscious awareness is crucial because most of your life experiences are filtered through your personal reality. If your personal filter system is brought to the surface, it will be possible to effect long-term changes of conditions and causes of your problematic patterns. (I define "personal reality" as your feelings, thoughts, behaviors, habits, and beliefs). When writing a personal inventory, the patterns of how you reacted to resentments, will help you understand your life on a much different level than you may have, up until this point.

The purpose of a Fourth Step Inventory (lists of your resentments, fears, sex conduct, and review of harms other than sexual), is to help you identify what character defects ("broken tools") continue to have power over your life experiences. Such character defects will continue to influence you until you call them into question. For example, it is very easy to say: *"I really want to stop this habit of lying to my spouse"*, (use your own examples) when in fact, you find it very hard to tell the truth. If you are not aware that it is hard for you to tell the truth, you will not be able to make a decision to change it.

The Fourth Step Inventory is a fact-finding, fact-facing, searching, detailed list that will disclose any flawed behavioral problems. It details your personal "reality". In order to sort out what you need to let go of (character defects: harmful, limiting, useless and outdated), you need to carefully examine *what is* your personal reality. Once that is disclosed you will be able to own your defects, and eventually let go of everything that is harmful (steps six through nine). Since our character defects run automatically twenty-four hours a day, you have to be completely committed to this process. If you are not completely committed to the process of sorting out and discarding your personal obstructions, you will remain a victim of your own limiting beliefs, thoughts, feelings, and habits. The goal when doing this inventory is to do it thoroughly and courageously.

SUGGESTED PRE-INVENTORY PRAYER

"My Creator, I invite you in to help me work openly, directly, intensely, and truthfully to write my personal inventory. I ask for your help in approaching my inventory with courage, strength, faith, grace, tolerance and patience, so I can discover what my personal stumbling blocks are. Help me to accept my past and present feelings and behaviors related to the trauma, and to help me change behaviors that are no longer useful. I no longer want to remain trapped with my secrets. Help me to have a more expanded view of myself, and to move through my fears as I set out to explore the real truth about myself. I ask for your Presence so I will not be overwhelmed or despair as a result of this discovery process. Amen."

The Fourth Step Inventory consists of four separate "inventories": 1 - Resentments, 2- Fears, 3-Sex Conduct, and 4-Harms done to others. Let us start with the Resentment Inventory (resentment is a re-feeling of anger whenever you think of something significant). Divide a sheet of paper into five columns, and label the columns as follows:

Column 1: Who or what am I resentful towards?

Column 2: What happened? (Or what did not happen, what did I not receive, or what was taken from me?)

Column 3: Which aspect of me was affected or violated? (Examples: self-esteem, pride, personal relationships, physical assets, and emotions).

Column 4: What did I do or not do? Here you are looking for your own mistakes, if there were any, to contribute to this situation. *If you were abused as a minor, state that. Children are never responsible for their abuse. If you were a victim and did not contribute to what happened, state that as well.*

Column 5: Which character-defect played a role in this? (If you were a child, or were completely innocent as an adult, just state that). Examples of "Character Defects" are: Selfish, Self-Seeking, Dishonest, Fearful, Inconsiderate, Withdrawn, Withholding, Stubborn, Lust, Negativity, Playing God, Controlling, Revenge, Prideful, Anger, Insecurity, Guilt, Needy, Self-Pity, Perfectionism, Irresponsible, Broken Word, Denial and Delusion, Compulsive, Impulsive, Greed, Jealous, Abusive. (Fill in anything that I left out here).

I suggest that you start out with your most intense resentments, and then proceed with the rest of your resentments. **REMINDER:** Step Four is about growth, moving forward and honest self-appraisal. If you are inclined toward self-blame and feel overcome by self-punishment, I suggest that you reach out for support. There is no growth or transformation in self-deprecation.

SAMPLE RESENTMENT INVENTORY

Column 1: Who or what am I resentful towards?	Column 2: What happened? (Or what did not happen, what did I not receive, or what was taken from me.)	Column 3: Which aspect of me was affected or violated? (Examples: self-esteem, pride, personal relationships, physical assets, and emotions.)	Column 4: What did I do or not do? (Your own mistakes, if there were any, to contribute to this situation.	Column 5: Which character-defect played a role in this?

A WORD ON FEAR

Fear is one of the four primal human emotions: fear, love, anger, and joy. Fear can be a gift and warn you of danger or a real problem that requires a solution. Fear can also be your own self-crafted illusion. Fear gets its supremacy to the extent that you avoid facing or feeling it. It also maintains its influence over you to the exact degree that you run away from it. Fear is often a gift because it reveals information that you need for your safety and security, and fear can also be debilitating. The goal of writing a Fear Inventory is to inquire in to the role of fear in your life, what are your specific fears, why you have these fears and how are they related to your resentments or dependency needs. And finally, are you willing to transform your fears into a trust for an Infinite Creator, and pray for guidance on what your Creator would have you be (opposite of your fears)?

SUGGESTED PRE-FEAR INVENTORY PRAYER

"Creative Intelligence, I thank you for supporting me through the process of being truthful with myself and my fears. Please provide me with clear direction on what I can, and cannot do with my fears, and guide me when I am triggered. I offer my fears to You, and ask You for Your Loving Guidance as I walk through them. I ask that you provide me with corrective experiences so I can outgrow my fears which no longer serve me. I ask for your strength so I will not be overwhelmed or despair as a result of this discovery process. Amen."

FORMAT OF FEAR INVENTORY

The Fear Inventory has the same format as the Resentment Inventory, with five columns.

Column One: Who or what do I fear? (List the names of people, institutions, principles, or situations).

Column Two: Why am I afraid? (What have they done to you, or will do to you? What do they symbolize for you?)

Column Three: Is this fear based on false or true information? If based on false information, can the fear be a result of your conditioning and learning, or a result of how you were impacted by the trauma?

Column Four: What is it that you want changed about this fear, that you will do whatever it TAKES?

Column Five: What is your new plan of action/inaction with regards to this fear?

SAMPLE FEAR INVENTORY

Column 1: Who or what do I fear?	Column 2: Why am I afraid?	Column 3: Is this fear based on false or true information?	Column 4: What is it that you want changed about this fear, that you will do whatever it TAKES?	Column 5: What is your new plan of action/inaction with regards to this fear?

SUGGESTED PRE-SEX INVENTORY PRAYER

*"Guiding Spirit, please help me face the reality of my past sexual relations. Grant me strength and courage to see where and how my sexual conduct has harmed myself and others. Help me to see, **and be connected,** to the truth of these relationships. I ask for the awareness of where I was at fault and what I could have done differently. I ask for your grace so I will not be overwhelmed or despair as a result of this discovery process. Amen."*

FORMAT OF SEX CONDUCT INVENTORY

The Review of Sex Conduct Inventory has the same format as the Resentment Inventory, with five columns.

Column One: Who did I hurt?

Column Two: What did I do, or not do, say or not say?

Column Three: Which part of me caused me to behave in this way? (Some examples include egoism, sex instinct, or social instinct.)

Column Four: How did my actions affect others? (Examples include: Jealousy, rage, suspicion, bitterness, pain, fear, agony, etc.) What would have been the ideal action to take instead? (Examples include: truth-telling, consideration, self-control, balanced perspective, etc).

Column Five: Which Character Defect played a role here? (Examples include: Selfish, dishonest, inconsiderate, self-seeking, frightened, impulsive, compulsive, stubborn, poor decision, etc.).

SAMPLE SEX CONDUCT INVENTORY

Column 1: Who did I hurt?	Column 2: What did I do, or not do, say or not say?	Column 3: Which part of me caused me to behave in this way?	Column 4: How did my actions affect others? **What would have been the ideal action to take instead?**	Column 5: Which Character Defect played a role here?

Trauma and Transformation: A 12-Step Guide.

REVIEW OF HARMS OTHER THAN SEXUAL

SUGGESTED PRAYER

"All Powerful Creator, I invite you to help me see where my behaviors or styles of interacting have caused harm to myself or others. Please grant me the willingness to give up my unacceptable behaviors that are harmful and keep me alienated from people. I am open to being taught appropriate behaviors, and I affirm my need to learn that it is acceptable for me to behave differently. I need and ask for Your help in my efforts to change. Please grace me with your Loving Kindness so that I will not be overwhelmed or despair as a result of this discovery process. Amen."

The Review of Harms Other Than Sexual has the same format as the Resentment Inventory, with five columns.

Column One: Who did I hurt?

Column Two: What did I do, or not do, say or not say? (Examples include: betray, lie, steal, cheat, revenge, manipulate, control, jealous, unforgiving, put people down, brake promises, withhold, irresponsible, engulfing, stifling, distant, etc).

Column Three: Which part of me caused me to behave in this way? (Examples include: Ego, sex instinct, social instinct, etc.)

Column Four: How did my actions affect them? (Examples include: Jealousy, rage, suspicion, bitterness, pain, fear, agony, etc.) What would have been the ideal response? (Examples include: truth-telling, consideration, self-control, fairness, modulate impulses, etc).

Column Five: Which Character Defect played a role here? (Examples include: Selfish, dishonest, inconsiderate, self-seeking, frightened, impulsive, compulsive, stubborn, poor decision-making, etc.).

SAMPLE INVENTORY FOR HARMS OTHER THAN SEXUAL

Column 1: Who did I hurt?	Column 2: What did I do, or not do, say or not say?	Column 3: Which part of me caused me to behave in this way?	Column 4: How did my actions affect others? **What would have been the ideal action to take instead?**	Column 5: Which Character Defect played a role here?

Step Four can be a time of discouragement as well as intense hope. If you were abused, you must exercise extreme caution before starting this step, and take the liberty to postpone it when you have all the resources you need to proceed. If you feel ready to begin this step, thoroughly check in with yourself if you are ready to withstand the pain this work will trigger, and seek additional help if necessary. You do not have to do this alone, and it is advisable to ask for support.

If you have everything you need to proceed, you should be aware that working on Step Four will most likely be the most painful work you will do in your recovery from trauma. This step entails recording the incidences of resentment that may have its roots in your traumatic experiences, the anger you may have never been aware of until now, the specific parts of your life that these resentments affected, and how you have been responding up until now. You dredge this all up, and re-experiencing those original feelings that most likely you have long-avoided, **in order to move beyond places where you may be stuck.**

The Fourth Step has the power to change lives, because if you can face the pain and uncover your authentic self (part or whole which may have gone underground as protection), you can use your pain as a tool for change. **<u>The question here is how well do you want to get?</u>** There are people that can give love, but reject receiving it, because they really do not want the connection. If you are one of those people, getting your resentments and anger out on paper, will accurately reveal in what areas your growth awaits you.

There are those people that discover through their Fourth Step Inventory, that they have been carrying around a hatred for a particular person, institution, or principles. If that applies to you, you will discover that hate is an extreme attachment to the need to be right. If you are resentful at having been traumatized *and blamed for it*, you may discover through your Inventory that you were not to blame and will slowly start to find relief from your pain and secrets. If you have the tendency to be selfish, you may discover that your Inventory leads you to answer the question: **"What does it look like when I am <u>un</u>selfish?"** This Inventory may lead you to a greater awareness with other people, and to be mindful how your behavior affects yourself and others.

If you struggled with intimate relationships, you may discover that you *"love"* but it is really a *dependency*, and therefore you are always consumed with worry if you were loved back or not. If you do the fourth column correctly ("Where was I selfish, dishonest, self-seeking, and frightened?") for each of the affected areas which were listed in column three, you may discover that where you most thought you were responsible, *you were not*, and where you did not think you were responsible, *you were* responsible.

You may be the one that discovers in your Inventory that your biggest resentment is in letting go of people, places or things, and that your pattern of letting go is either with claw marks, or by withdrawing. Some people discover that their learned way of relating to others is by rushing in and trying to rescue people, and cannot listen to another person without the urge to rush in and fix the person. This particular pattern of relating to others, like all other dysfunctional patterns, needs to be unlearned, which takes time and process. These are some of the examples of personal discoveries from people that have worked the Fourth Step. **They discovered that they have options other than long-held behavioral patterns that stem from unresolved trauma.**

POST-INVENTORY FOLLOW UP

Resentment, as previously described, is when you remember a particular incident and you feel anger. You can imagine a red flag going up every time you are having resentment. After you do a Fourth Step Inventory about it, you can test to see if you still have resentment. Think about it, and notice if the Red Flag of Resentment is either up or down. (I do not want to falsely present Step Four as a magic pill that will erase resentments. However, there is something very powerful about getting YOUR story out on paper and reviewing it in a systematic and analytical way, with the intent for spiritual transformation. Sometimes a shift in perspective can occur just by letting out the pain and grief. There are some things that will always be a sore point, and no amount of inventorying will make a difference. That is okay. The point is to get out the anger in a way that is safe, organized, and concrete).

No one wants to experience a trauma, even if it does provide an excellent situation at some point for profound spiritual growth. There is no sufficient consolation for the survivor who experienced shattering childhood sexual abuse, death of a beloved parent, physical abuse of a parent, acts of terrorism, a painful divorce, illness, accidents or painful separations. Perhaps you go through life shut down and only vaguely know that you are anxious, miserable or depressed. Any trauma can leave you feeling resentful or can trigger you to act-out against yourself or others. A barrier to writing a fourth step inventory is if you think that the resulting information or insight will be too painful and self-knowledge means condemnation. Self–knowledge will *not* shelter you from pain, and insight allows you to see yourself and your personal story with a more evolved, accurate perspective.

The change from this step comes as a result of action, and if you cannot see something in your life, you may not be ready to see it. That applies here as well. Everyone has "blind spots", and in those areas you will not be able to cope with something that you cannot see. This work requires a lot of emotional courage, especially if you have never conducted a thorough self-examination. You may begin your personal Inventory feeling that every one of your personal character defects are because of *someone else.* The truth is that these defects would have caused you trouble anywhere. Some people prefer to see their character defects as "emotional wounds that cause inner burns", or as "defensive operations". However you choose to call it, the main thing is that you get help with your process. I can safely assure you that you will slowly start to find relief as a result of your digging and excavating, and you will also learn new strengths to meet the challenge of shedding old skin.

THE FOURTH STEP AS A LAMP

I see Step Four as a lamp that never burns out. It is always there for my use but only when I choose to see things with clarity and awareness. The main benefit for me with Step

Four was relief from shame, guilt, and trust difficulties. I got to know and understand myself from a compassionate perspective. **The personal inventory *is not* designed to be a story book about one's long-forgotten personal history, feelings, attitudes, behaviors, and ways of coping.** It is designed for you to get relief and understanding for your intense resentments, fears, guilt, and blockages. In my personal efforts to be searching and fearless from the very start, in effect, I was turning on a light in a very dark prison cell, and I found a way out. My truth was a lamp that lit the room to see that there was an exit door, and I was not being held prisoner. I thought that this prison cell had a permanently sealed door, but with the lamp, I was able to see it was unlocked the whole time. **With denial no longer operating, the prison cell door opened with the help of my earnestness, efforts and prayer.** At the same time of doing this inventory, I began a huge housecleaning, throwing out all of my unwanted, outdated clutter. I began to make room for something new both in my psyche and in my home. I felt a new kind of Presence in the clear, clean space that I just created. The most common example used in Twelve Step meetings to describe the necessity of Step Four is of a store owner that carefully reviews her records to see what is in stock, what is missing, and what needs to be upgraded, replaced or gotten rid of altogether. **Using the information you learn from taking this step, you can see what your stumbling blocks are, where they are located, and to proactively remove them before you repeat your cycle.**

WHAT'S MORALITY GOT TO DO WITH IT?!

Writing an inventory would have seemed a lot less threatening to me were it not for the word *moral,* implying that I was looking for everything that is wrong with me. I thought this step was about harsh judgment. Upon further reflection, however, the two descriptive words that most resonate with me for "moral" are *clean* and *ethical*.

This step calls for self-love and an honoring of one's hurts (origin of resentment). It is also a chance to come clean about your role in the conflicts that may have caused some of your resentments. When you come clean about your part, if you had any role in your resentments, you may have a shift in perspective. What you decide to do with this new shift will be determined by your working through the rest of the Twelve Steps.

The exploration in Step Four is a delicate process. Destructive, or otherwise painful behavioral patterns are usually rooted in unresolved pain and misunderstanding. Without the lens of compassion, you can stop this process from being a relief to you, or you can cause further harm. I took this opportunity of writing my inventories to look deeper in myself to find the source of my patterns, and have since found healthier ways of expressing my feelings, wants and needs. Although the source of my defensive behavior was rooted in a childhood over which I had no control over, it was no longer an excuse to continue utilizing them. I knew where the exit door was and walked out a free woman. The morality of this process (clean, honest, good, and ethical) is the linchpin of writing a successful inventory.

I cannot stress enough the importance of being compassionate toward yourself when writing your inventory. For this process to be effective, you must be willing to admit what maladaptive coping mechanisms are no longer working in your life. You may have destructive tendencies that keep you from having loving connections with yourself and others. Analyzing your patterns and evaluating what behaviors, attitudes and thoughts you would like to stop, will significantly change the way you operate in the world.

The key is to have a balanced and compassionate perspective. This is not about self-blame, but it is about taking healthy, appropriate responsibility where needed. It can seem terrifying to think of the traumatic experiences you survived and how it affected your life. Admitting responsibility for forming coping mechanisms can seem like a forced confession, and this guilt can hinder you from healing your shame. In my case, I arrived at a profound self-knowledge of why I behaved in the ways that I did, and although it was a response to threats in my childhood environment, I no longer wanted to respond in such unhealthy ways. I affirmed that I did the best I could, considering what I had to work with, and *I was now perfectly capable to make different choices*. This did not mean that I no longer carried the scars of painful events, but rather, I was becoming more responsible for my life in the present. This was a turning point in my journey. It is not healthy for anyone to see themselves only as a victim, yet you still need to acknowledge the effects that traumatic events had on your life, your psyche, your personality and your well-being.

My friend Rachel completed her fourth step inventory and felt she was in a crisis. She felt a sense of futility and despair, as if trapped with no way out. She faced her years of emotional neglect and abuse, and realized she was living a life pretending none of this happened. She felt chronically depressed or angry most of the time, and by viewing her inventory, she made a decision to no longer avoid the negative truths in her life. She used her inventory to admit these truths and to define her problems clearly. Step Four calls for "fearlessness" and for Rachel this meant that she would not let her fear stop her from facing her issues and working on them in therapy. Some of the unpleasant issues that she faced in herself were her tendencies to overreact, wallow in self-pity instead of taking action, and respond narcissistically. She looked at her narcissism and her tendency to engulf others and harbor jealous obsessions. Initially, Rachel felt worse before she felt better, because she had to first express her negative feelings about her life, as the first critical step for to begin her transformation.

Without the honest expression that Step Four calls for, the rest of the Twelve Steps will be inadequate because you will continue to repress the real underlying issues. This kind of fearless inventory allows you to pick up the most difficult feelings that can arise from a "fearless, moral inventory" and to wrestle with it; to get to know it, and to face it head-on. The benefits of this emotional effort include increased inner peace, can prevent re-victimization and will make you aware of why you are miserable (as you have previously self-identified in Step One). It also illuminates the direction for your solutions.

The most significant moment in each step, is when you wake up. At a certain moment, you become conscious of your imprisoned state and you decide how you are going to orchestrate your escape. You begin by letting go of your story of self-blame. This is followed by becoming increasingly conscious and aware; a process many survivors naturally fight against, because that consciousness will awaken misery and entrapment. **But the payoff is that you also become aware of your options which are hopefully based on your True Self.**

CONSCIOUSNESS RISING

To discover whether you need to deal with your traumatic past and if the Fourth Step Inventory can help you in your growth process, ask yourself the following questions about your life, and then write your answers below.

Trauma and Transformation: A 12-Step Guide.

Do you question the meaning of life, because of what you survived? Describe.

_____

_____

_____

_____

Do you want to clearly understand the meanings and origins of your trauma-reactive habits, irrational behaviors, attitudes and symptoms? The payoff to gaining this knowledge is a relief from painful symptoms such as anxiety, depression, and blocks to making valuable changes in your life.

_____

_____

_____

_____

Are you an adult victim of child abuse where your internal "emotional circuits" were weakened or damaged by chronically inflamed fear and rage during extensive periods of your upbringing? If yes, do you feel overwhelmed at times emotionally, and utilize your character defects as a way to cope?

_____

_____

_____

_____

Do you forget things automatically (unconsciously), when you feel threatened, specifically when the intensity of your guilt, fear, depression or anxiety gets too great for you? (This is an unconscious defense).

_____

_____

_____

_____

Are you living in a family, or working in a job, that takes up all of your energy but you don't experience it as giving back what *you* need?

_____

_____

_____

_____

Do you feel an internal pressure to please others, and does this "people pleasing" hold you from growing? (Do you passively let other people make your decisions?)

_____

_____

_____

_____

Do you let other people take credit for what you have done? If yes, why do you allow for that? (Examples include: fear, inaccurate self-esteem, and chronic emotional pain, and revenge, lack of good role models, confusion, or ignorance?)

_____

_____

_____

Can you not seem to be rid of the excessive guilt and shame you carry?

_____

_____

_____

_____

Do you wish you could avoid destructive relationships but act on your compulsion to keep repeating the same destructive pattern over and over again ("repetition-compulsion")?

_____

_____

_____

What are your personal methods of keeping yourself from experiencing your emotions? Are your methods maladaptive?

_____

_____

_____

Do you want to trade this in for a more healthy and loving way of relating to yourself and others?

_____

_____

_____

_____

Do you try *too* hard, or not enough, to connect with others? If yes, how does this make you feel, and view other people?

_____

_____

_____

_____

Do you feel the desire to be restored to spiritual integrity? If yes, what is motivating you?

_____

_____

_____

_____

It is imperative that you take a look at your gifts, skills, assets and positive contributions. This is all part of becoming conscious and aware of what has had a positive impact on your life and on the lives of others. Step Four is about having an accurate picture of yourself, and not just a one sided lamentation over hurts and suffering from the past. This includes the character traits and behaviors you want more of. A close friend of mine, Susan Price, L.M.S.W., refers to this as the *Garden of Eden Theory*. She explains that a stuck person needs to visit the Garden of Eden to find out what it feels like to feel good. Once you visit those parts of yourself that are healthy, and you partake of pleasure in your divinely ordained attributes, you realize what is *not* working and what *is* working in your life. You need to have such a contrast in order to have a clear perception of yourself. With this combination of hope and discomfort in what you see in yourself, you create a climate for appropriate change. This change brings about an increase in self-awareness. This is not to be confused with self-absorption, narcissism or self-centeredness. The difference is in the process of consciousness rising, an attitude of love and tolerance, using self-knowledge to take the next right action, and regular spiritual practice and growth.

SUGGESTED PRAYER FOR ASSETS AND GIFTS INVENTORY

"My Creator, I invite you in to help me uncover, discover, and recover my personal assets and gifts. I ask for your help in approaching my blessings with courage, humility, strength, integrity, and joy, so I can utilize them in the service of humanity. Help me to accept them, and grant me the strength to help make this world a better place, in partnership with you. I no longer want to remain trapped and in hiding with my blessings. Please help me to have a more accurate view of myself, and to awaken to the Real Me, as you originally created me. I ask for your Presence so I will not shy away from, or be overwhelmed with this process. Amen."

SAMPLE INVENTORY OF ASSESTS, GIFTS, AND BLESSINGS

Column 1 What brings me the greatest joy?	**Column 2** What am I naturally drawn to, that occupies my thoughts, time, and fantasies?	**Column 3** What do I yearn for the most?	**Column 4** What am I really good at?	**Column 5** List all of your positive qualities. Spend a minimum of 20 minutes writing out this list.

Please be patient with your process of awakening. If you are just waking up from a long and deep slumber, remember that a rising consciousness takes time and patience. Your new-found self-respect and self-acceptance will help you spring out of your personal traps, and with that, you have a raised capacity for utilizing your blessings and gifts for transformation. This is possible regardless of what was done to you, or what you have personally suffered. This is the essence of emotional liberation, a painstaking process requiring patience, love, prayer and compassion.

Life is full of suffering, and it is also full of the overcoming of it.
-HELEN KELLER

I am a passionate seeker after truth which is but another name for God.
-GANDHI

STEP 5

Admitted to God, to ourselves and to another human being the exact nature of our wrongs.

At first glance, you may feel absolutely resistant when you look at this step. *How can I let someone find out about me?* You may feel fear, dread, anticipation of rejection and humiliation if anyone knows of your past or "secrets". Perhaps you may feel knots and tangles in your body with no vision or understanding as to how to "untangle" those knots. "Fearlessly" writing an inventory takes enough energy, and trips your trigger wires badly enough – now you have to actually *share this with someone.* When I got ready to share my inventory with my beloved therapist, I was pleasantly surprised when I discovered that this process became the validation I had always longed for. The much-needed validation I got was for the long list of incidents I listed in my resentments that I had no responsibility for. I also got the support to change what I could change, and I increased in wisdom to know what I cannot change (serenity prayer). I got the reassurance that I had the strength and courage to change whatever patterns I was ready to look at. The experience of working through the grief, a vital part of this experience, brought me to "admitting" to my Healing Power (God) that I was hurting and wanted a different way to respond to life.

This was an enormously empowering experience as I believed that my emotional isolation was coming to an end. I began to feel a sense of connectedness that was fundamentally different to what I was used to. The way that I had internalized both the trauma I experienced, and the maladaptive behavioral habits, created a core of shame that kept me feeling like I must remain in hiding. At this point, my shame began to lift as it was *"brought to the light of consciousness"*. My therapist was "another human being" that helped me to see *the exact nature of my wrongs,* and how to resolve the inner conflicts that fueled those responses and behaviors. She helped me to understand that "wrongs" are also symbols for how I have shortchanged myself, or have been lacking in knowledge and acceptance. Life is lived on a much higher and more satisfying plane when the truth is told, feelings are felt, and behavior is loving and respectful towards self, others, and humanity in general.

The fourth and fifth steps are about truth-telling with the God of your understanding, and another safe person. For some, this may be the first time you have ever done something like this. For me, it certainly was. I did not expect the compassion and empathy that I received. I was also unaware, until that point, how the truth combined with right action, can be powerful enough to triumph over and repair the damage of destructive secrets and lies.

If this all sounds too much, not believable, or too scary, please be assured that your reaction is perfectly natural! Perhaps there is a tiny voice inside you that is curious, to some degree, if this can work for you too. I would suggest simply having a safe and neutral friend listen to the parts of your life you keep under a tight lock and key. If you have a safe, neutral person who will respect your trust and privacy, and is available to listen, take the risk.

As you relate your fifth step inventory, try to access the feelings that match it. Where there is emotion during a process there is investment, so I encourage you to express yourself with appropriate affect. You do not need someone to be a perfect listener, nor to completely understand or identify with what you went through. The key is that they are available to offer you a presence that is nonjudgmental, safe, and present. In my case, I chose to share all of it with my therapist with whom I still have a continuing safe and trusting relationship. This has made all of the difference, and impacted my life very significantly. Every survivor needs a loving and competent mentor. I support you in seeking out such a person, and if you are well qualified (mentally, emotionally, and spiritually) to become a mentor yourself, I support you in seeking students. This teacher-student relationship is the channel responsible for the transmission of knowledge, healing and recovery. If you are not yet a part of it, you are duly invited to become a part of this holy process!

RETURN TO PAIN AND HEAL THE SHAME

Everyone experiences trauma differently, and the effect and nature of the damage is very personal. **However, if you feel you have *no choice* but to keep something a secret, those are the most crucial items to be shared. For some people, hanging on to the secret, and therefore the**

shame, may be about protecting *someone else's* bad behavior. For a lot of survivors of trauma, there is an element of confused loyalty, and therefore, a maladaptive desire to protect something or someone related to what happened. If you identify with this, you may want to consider that your resistance to sharing certain resentments (returning to the pain), is because you are holding on to *someone else's secret,* and therefore have **become a carrier of their shame.** By internalizing this shame, in some way, you "cooperate" and perhaps even unjustifiable blame yourself. This internalization lets the perpetrator of the trauma "off the hook", since you are carrying inside what actually belongs to them (shame, guilt, remorse).

As long as you are carrying secrets, you are still in control of the event or person. When you "turn it over" to another safe person, the termination of secrecy will validate that stifled message. In many ways, you are not unique, because there are so many trauma survivors who are on the journey for recovery. When you keep secrets (the opposite of Step Five), you feel isolated, unique, and alone in your story.

It does not matter if you share parts of your story with more than one person, but it is important that your story does not remain in hiding. If you keep parts of *your story* in hiding, *you remain there as well.* In various ways, the shame and guilt, kept alive by its attending secrets, is more harmful than the actual trauma. This is because the secrecy does not allow for any reality-checks on the feelings of self-doubt, confusion, and sense of powerlessness. You end up living a life with an underlying reality that controls *you* twenty-four hours a day. However, when you are ready to honestly share your truth, be certain to choose someone who will not personalize what you reveal. For example, **family members, partners or children are usually not the best people to hear this kind**

of material. In sharing what you remember of your traumatic past and your coping mechanisms, you may gain two valuable gifts: 1- the long-awaited-for validation and support, so that you can reconnect to those dissociated parts of yourself, and 2- a more realistic perspective on what happened, so that you can finally let go of unnecessary self-blame, shame and guilt.

The main gift of the Fifth Step for me was a radical shift in how I related to myself. Feelings that were once too overwhelming were now tangled places inside me that simply needed love, space and compassion. The fear of approaching the Fourth and Fifth Steps is understandable because most of us do not have any experience in bearing our souls on such an intimate level. There is an expression in the Twelve Step rooms that describes the purpose of this process of going to a deep level, in order to "uncover, discover and recover". This is also known as "peeling of the onion", a slow process that takes time, dedication, perseverance and patience. Like most survivors, you may have closely guarded secrets of which you are terrified will be revealed.

In my step work, I was able to identify them as frozen feelings and memories that had never been brought to the light. I brought them to the light, in part, by getting them down on paper and then sharing them. The relief I felt, and my gratitude in being taught how to do this, is difficult to describe in words. My long-held belief that I must hide my secrets that haunted me for so long was beginning to melt away.

Survivors may avoid re-experiencing their story, and the attending emotions (e.g., anger, fear, pain, shame, loneliness, and a sense of helplessness). Step Five is an *incredible opportunity for "grief work"*, and letting go of your burdens: conscious and unconscious; buried, and unheard. Step Five helped me to experience deeper intimacy with myself, with one definition of intimacy as: *"in to me you see"*. This relief is available to any survivor who is willing to be candid and patient with their process.

One of my biggest fears in discovering my "inner stuck-points" was about not being supported or believed. However, I stopped doubting myself, and stayed with the process of Step Five, this fear did not materialize because I shared my story with the right person(s) and it eventually dissipated. I believed what I remembered, cognitively, physically and emotionally, and I discovered that my healing began *with validating my own experiences and pain*. What followed this was a journey back to reconnecting *to myself*. When I made a commitment *to honor my truth*, to seek out what was previously hidden and to truly "clean house" psychologically, I felt intense relief and a sense of wonderment and hope. The discovery was so liberating!

If you experience fear at the thought of Step Five, soothe yourself the way you once needed to be soothed but were not. What did you need to hear? Take a moment right now to write that down, and then say it out loud. What feelings or sensations come up for you? In the aftermath of surviving a trauma, there is an enormous need for reassurance, compassion, relief and safety.

_____

_____

_____

_____

Perhaps you never had such an open and intimate experience with anyone. Awakening to your reality, feelings, needs, defects, gifts, attributes, etc (all the result of Steps Four and Five), can terrify you, let alone sharing them with someone else, no matter how much you trust them! The Twelve Steps, especially the Fourth and Fifth step is not for the faint of heart. However, it is well-worth extending yourself the self-love and compassion to reach out to a safe person to hear your Fifth Step with attention, time, and patience.

ADMITTED TO GOD

There are two powerful interactions with this step: your connection with "another person" and your connection to God (use any word that is personal to you). When you *"admit to God"*, you allow for an unguarded communication with your Source. For some people, you may have never done something like this before; for others, this may be a regular spiritual practice. A potential obstacle can be a harboring of resentment, anger, or distrust for authority figures, which may naturally extend to a Higher Power. Such fear and resentment is easy to project on to God; a Being you cannot directly see or engage with, as you would a person of flesh and blood. Admitting this all may feel futile, at first glance, if you blame a Higher Power for the tragedies that you or others experienced. If that is the case, you are not alone. **Let this be the chance for you to say exactly what you always wanted to say.** It helps me to remember that a sincere heart opens many doors.

INTIMATE COMMUNICATION WITH A HIGHER POWER

The following exercise may not be easy for you to do, because you will have to really "dredge up" what you are so sore about, and its connection to a power far greater than your limited human understanding. How can such an exercise be simple? It is not. However, it will lead you to precise inner "surgery", so that you can remove some toxic beliefs about the roles and responsibilities of those involved in your trauma. It is definitely worth a try!

Trauma and Transformation: A 12-Step Guide.

What have you always wanted to say to a Higher Power?

What happened that caused you to reject the concept of a loving Higher Power? (BE HONEST AND OPEN!)	What do you REALLY want to say to God about your trauma, your feelings and beliefs about it?	What responsibility to you assign to this Higher Power, which may belong to the actual perpetrator (Man's Will versus God's Will)?	Having said ALL OF IT, how do you feel in the present moment?

Through a long, detailed and patient process, I came to know and accept that the fundamental reality of **_human self-will_** is responsible for my traumatic experiences. The question of *"why do bad things happen to good people"*, remains unanswered and a topic of great tension. Throughout human history, humans have tried to make peace with their explanations. I personally do not have the answer. What I do have, however, is overwhelming evidence *in my life*, revealing the loving presence of a Higher Power, who protected me through it all. This may seem like a contradiction, and I arrived at this conclusion by actively and deliberately seeking the hidden blessings in everything. What about you? Can you take some time, right now, to recall the times, places, and incidences in which you felt or witnessed this Presence?

_____

_____

_____

_____

I would like to answer the question that you may have at this moment: just *how* exactly does a trauma survivor "*admit to God the exact nature of our wrongs*"? I will share with you a story that may answer this question.

Benjamin grew up in a remote village in Ireland. He was a simple individual who would not consider himself religious in any sense. Although he was raised in a very strict Catholic home, he rejected religion, and remained suspicious of authority figures and organized religion. According to his understanding, God was simply an Awakening. Benjamin experienced this Awakening wherever he went, and all around him, but this did not come easy for him.

Sadly, Benjamin came from a family where truth was not encouraged or welcomed. Often he was punished for his truthfulness, vulnerability, and openness. As a consequence, he spent many years isolated and fearful of people. When he first read this step, he froze. This kind of trust and deep connection was unfathomable to him. I suggested to him that he take walks in the forest, and converse with this Spirit, the way he would with a close companion. Not as a confessional, but to simply speak the truth of his heart. Benjamin described the awkwardness of attempting this, but did not give up because "*I felt something shift inside but I can't really explain what or why.*" He now practices his Fourth and Fifth Step regularly. In his own words, he explained to me that through this process he purged a lot of the toxic shame and guilt he had no clue was buried inside of him.

My close friend Chava's religious affiliation is as a Chassidic, ultra-orthodox Jew. She prays at least twice a day, using a traditional Hebrew prayer book. Chava describes her Fifth Step as "*my silent prayer in my heart where I whisper to Hashem (God) everything I need to embrace and let go of*". For Chava, she feels fulfilled and connected to God, during her twice daily prayers. Personalizing her communication with God relieves her burdens, and enhances her experience of having a direct line with her Creator.

Boaz, a young Israeli soldier, had not been able to accept that there was a God. He attributed this to all of the horror and violence that he was surrounded with growing up near the Gaza Strip, Israel. He expressed feeling *"very guilty because of my Jewish religious upbringing and love for my country"*. Boaz describes this struggle as *"a fog where I cannot see through the other side to an unconditional loving God. I just saw too much in my life and I don't believe. I will never get past this. Period"*. When he shared his Fourth Step inventory with a roommate, whom he trusted, he reported feeling understood and supported unconditionally. He attributes that moment of heart-felt human understanding as the starting point where he understood "God" as a *"strong heart-to-heart connection*". This felt-experience guided him through his ongoing process of transformation.

Through the Fifth Step, I had a deeper experience of Step Two (*"...came to believe in a power greater than ourselves"*). I *"came to believe"* through felt experience that I was not isolated and not alone. This Power knocked on the castle gates and laid out a bridge for me to come out of my Tower of Isolation. The knocking appeared in many different forms, including through my own intuition, people, places, and things that were deliberately and wisely placed right outside of the castle gates.

I had started to cherish this new-found sense of intimacy and belonging, and began a regular spiritual practice of *"admitting to God."* Communion on this level can come with difficulty for some survivors, if you are used to being emotionally withdrawn or shut-down. Bear in mind throughout the entire process, **that the only right way to do a Fifth Step is with an honest heart, and with the appropriate parties**, as previously explained. You will then be a co-creator of compassion and intimacy with yourself and another person.

Call upon God by any reasonable name you wish because the name is not important. What is important is facing a possible reality of yours: that you may have gone your whole life longing for this exact connection, and this has been your missing link to fulfillment. *It does not have to remain an unfulfilled yearning.* I venture to speculate that an untold number of people go through life deeply desiring this kind of intimacy, with God and another human being, but are blocked in various ways from accomplishing this.

As you saw in the stories of Benjamin and Boaz, a common roadblock to accomplishing the kind of intimacy and connection that Step Five calls for is the emotional risk it entails. For these men, like for countless other survivors, it is also the end of isolation and fear of truth-telling. Where it used to be true that telling the truth came with a heavy, undesirable price, it now comes with a huge reward: relief.

THE EXACT NATURE OF OUR WRONGS

At this point, you may think to yourself: "*Alright, this seems worthwhile trying, so I'll give it a shot. But what about:* "**the exact nature of my wrongs**"? *What have I done? I survived a trauma, that's all. I don't need a confessional! Must I admit to a 'wrong' for it to work?*" Great question! I had the same question, and my beloved friend Shannon answered it when he suggested I view the word *"wrongs"* as *"broken tools"*. For example, in my inventory I found that my primary "broken tool" was emotional hiding. I typically did not consciously outright lie, but had a very hard time in being direct, open, and matching my words with my heart's reality. I was trained to keep secrets, deny my needs, not ask for what I wanted or needed, and remain fearful and inappropriately compliant. I felt enormous relief to identify one of my core character defects/"broken tool", which was keeping me from meaningful relationships. So I began to tally up my strengths and limitations, and for every limitation, I found a strength of equal power. The Fifth Step was my opportunity to no longer minimize the difficult parts of my story and to let go of the need to stay in hiding.

The crucial part of the Fifth Step process is to make sure that your Fifth Step is *not* simply a reading of your Step Four Inventories. Instead, the focus is on what you are admitting, which is the *"exact nature of our wrongs"* (your "broken tools" that enable your particular problematic behaviors). The purpose is to see clearly why you acted in the ways that you did that caused harm to yourself and/or to another person. If you are still having trouble identifying these, think back to your role in troubling situations that seem to repeat in your life ("*repetition compulsion*"). It is in these repeated patterns that you will find the answer to this question. The key to identifying the *"exact nature of our wrongs"* is in identifying the common thread in your patterns.

Use the chart below to explore how your character defects have kept you troubled in some way. Ask yourself: How has your character defects contributed to your chronic loneliness, addictions and compulsions, unmanageability in life, or unfulfilled relationships?

Trauma and Transformation: A 12-Step Guide.

EXERCISE IN EVALUATING THE USEFULNES S OF YOUR CHARACTER DEFECTS

My Primary "Broken Tools" are:	How have these "Broken Tools" helped me at one point in my life – but are NOW my Road Blocks?	What would happen to my current problematic patterns if I put down this "Broken Tool" and replace it with a functional, appropriate one?

Some trauma survivors repeat patterns of abuse, and become perpetrators on other people. This can be intentional or unintentional. Survivors often experience emotional numbness, and may not be aware that they are falling short by not being fully connected to oneself. Survivor guilt, shame, and other intense feelings, unprocessed, is a large intense burden. Most likely, this burden will not just go away on its own.

Practicing **courage**, as one of the four spiritual principles that Step Five calls for (the other three are **self-honesty, commitment, and trust**), is very necessary in order to honestly share *your entire* inventory. Perhaps this is the first time in your life you have thought of yourself as courageous, honest, committed or trustworthy. These four qualities are the four golden spiritual tickets required, in order to enter into the inner palace which your true self calls "home".

When I shared my Fifth Step with my therapist, I was able to let go of a lot of the shame that typically accompanies traumatic and abusive experiences. This energy was now freed for the first time in my life, and I no longer had to carry a burden that was unhealthy and therefore unproductive. Taking Step Four without "turning it over" (Step Five), would eliminate that gut-level, intimate sharing. Had I skipped Step Five, I would live a life dominated by false beliefs about myself, about my role in certain circumstances, and about traumatic events in general.

Having survived trauma did not create a "wrong" in me, but rather, I adopted maladaptive coping mechanisms to survive. I discovered and accepted that these were no longer necessary or helpful. I now had a connection to, and relationship with, a <u>power much greater than</u> my perpetrator(s), traumata I went through, wounds I

suffered, and hurts that were deeply embedded inside of me - to help me tell my private, embarrassing secrets.
Step Five also awakened gratitude in me for being a survivor. It gave me legitimate reason to forgive and let go of everything I had no control over. I define "forgive" as a simple acceptance that whatever happened *was real*, that certain people did what they did, made *their* choices, and that I no longer have to use my broken tools to respond to overwhelming or uncomfortable situations, as I was once trained to do.

Taking the Fifth Step afforded me the clarity and insight to see both sides of my story; where I had been wounded, and where I was continuing to tell my story through the utilization of broken and outdated tools. This is not a moral issue, and is in fact, the way that humans are wired. The clinical concept for *"character defect"* can also be referenced as *"defense mechanism"*, and it has saved many lives. Armed with my new insights, I began to practice being compassionate, open and truthful on a more evolved level. While this was done imperfectly, it was my beginning for developing genuine closeness with safe others.

LONG-TERM EFFECTS OF TRAUMA AS STUMBLING BLOCKS TO A FIFTH STEP

There are some forms of trauma that for some people time will not cure. Depending on the person, and on the specific trauma, or traumata (multiple traumas experienced), the consequences flourish, although the memories may have gone into hiding. The effects show up as self-destructive behavior of various sorts (perpetrating abuse, addictions, compulsions, chronic hiding, etc). These effects of trauma are always there, waiting for clarity of consciousness, immediately followed by the right interventions. This all flows from an intimate sharing with a safe other. Although this level of connecting can initially feel uncomfortable, even anxiety-producing, you need corrective experiences of intimate connection, just like everyone else.

Taking Step Five has the power to help you end the pattern of thought that you are *"too damaged"* to stop reacting from your wound-space. This is because when you face your secrets, guilt, shame, pain and self-doubt with another safe person who accepts you, you allow yourself to receive unconditional love. I believe that on some level, every survivor wishes they were not wounded or affected by what happened. This subconscious wish may also lead survivors to feel a lot of pressure to look or act "normal".

When one has been personally wounded in some significant way, acting on this pressure can lead to a false existence. Step Five is about sharing the most real, and perhaps the most hidden parts of you. This can be very liberating, but you have to experience it for yourself, in order to believe the words you are reading. Unfortunately, you live in a society that provides you with ample reason to avoid all this. Healing from trauma, revealing your "secrets", working on character defects, replacing "broken tools" with healthy behaviors, etc, are not on the forefront of society's to-do list. You are bombarded with messages from the media about how you should look, act, dress, earn, and what is your overall worth. This causes fear-based thinking, feeling, and believing; perhaps going through your entire life span anticipating, and avoiding, societal rejection. Or perhaps you hold on tight to society's messages of materialism, and really do not care if you "heal", or if you are spiritually fit. Either way, you burden yourself by expecting to keep the secrets buried, keep the pain at bay, and maintain a certain front.

You cannot live a full, deep, free, and meaningful life if you are always looking over your shoulder to see which hungry ghost from the past is still chasing you. Metaphorically speaking, if you anxiously try to protect your secrets, character defects, and wounds', making sure no one looks long enough, you never do let them go.

REVIEW AND MOVING ON

1. In what ways, if any, have I avoided being honest and intimate with myself, God, and other people?

_____

_____

_____

_____

2. Has the Fifth Step helped me to practice self-honesty?

_____

_____

_____

_____

3. Is there any relationship between self-honesty, and self acceptance? What is it?

_____

_____

_____

_____

4. As a result of taking the Fifth Step, have I developed an internal picture of myself and of my Higher Power that will contribute to a commitment to my development?

_____

_____

_____

_____

Trauma and Transformation: A 12-Step Guide.

5. Did my view of myself and my story begin to shift as a result of Step Five?

_____

_____

_____

_____

"When you tell your trouble to your neighbor you present him with a part of your heart. If he possesses a great soul, he thanks you; if he possesses a small one, he belittles you." [5]

---

[5] Gibran, Kahlil. *The Treasured Writings of Kahlil Gibran*, (New York: Castle Books, 2010), Pg. 57.

STEP SIX

Were entirely ready to have God remove all these defects of character.

When I first attempted this step, I had two immediate thoughts: 1) How and why would my Higher Power "remove" anything from me, and 2) What would I feel like if I were "entirely ready" to give up all my "defects"? I felt that if I would attempt this step, I would allow something extreme in my life, and this seemed intimidating. My fear was that Step Six meant I would have to open up in a way that felt unnatural to me. Frankly, I did not want to let go of what I thought would have to be too much, too fast, or parting from my vital survival skills. Taking this step did not seem at all appealing to me.

The way I processed my fears was by asking which parts of me I thought would be removed, and was I afraid of having to live a life without these very necessary parts of myself. My fear was that this meant I had to become someone fundamentally different from my basic personality and nature. This was because I believed that I was defective, and who I was must be problematic. This too, is another tragic result of trauma and victimization. It is *not* the intent of Step Six at all.

TRAUMA-REACTIVE HABITS

Once I had some experience with Step Six, I learned that my character defects, such as emotional hiding, can be transformed through courage, so that I can speak my truth and ask for what I need. I was not going to suddenly become an entirely different person; I was simply going to transform a trauma-reactive habit (hiding), into a strength-based quality (speaking my truth, and advocating for my needs). I also became ready to explore ways that my personal trauma-reactive habits were manifesting in my life, and were no longer serving me. One way to evaluate this for yourself is by asking this question: *"In what areas of my life do I deprive myself unnecessarily, consume far beyond what I need, or repeat the same unhealthy or destructive habits?"* Answer this question in the space that follows.

_____

_____

_____

_____

If you are one of those people who cling to their shortcomings with frightening stubbornness, not looking for solutions and blaming everyone else, taking Steps Six and Seven is non-negotiable if you truly desire emotional and spiritual recovery. It is a well-known fact in the mental health profession, and in the self-help arena, that without spiritual and emotional recovery, a survivor experiences life that is constricted, lacking spirit. By choosing to take responsibility for your spiritual recovery from trauma, you align yourself to an authentic purpose and vision for your life. The general rule is that you get what you work for. This recovery process is void of magic, and filled with God's Grace. You will *not* be struck free from core character traits. However, if you take the initiative to stop practicing character defects, and work in cooperation with your Higher Power, they can be removed from you.

Upon close examination, this step asks only that you become *ready*. This readiness will set you up to search for a new way to live, to be in the world, to think and behave, and to relate to other people. Learning about the concept of "readiness" helped me to realize that I did *not* feel ready, and that I believed I *could not* change certain character defects in me. This is where the words..."*to have God remove*"... lightened up my dismal picture. Since character defects are a part of a person, and will probably resurface under stressful conditions, I had to do what I did in Step One and in Step Two. I had to admit that there are some very intense triggers inside of me, and that I need something much Greater to provide insight and relief. I understand the word "remove" as not a literal hand reaching inside of me and taking something physical away from me, but rather, intuitive guidance, relief, and a cognitive restructuring where necessary. For example, I asked to have my limiting beliefs about love and relationships removed from me. These beliefs fueled my character defect of fear, and after I prayed for this removal in Step Six, I felt a strong sense of relief.

I saw my limiting beliefs as just that: limiting. I restructured these beliefs as something that was handed down to me, but I now have the choice to re-examine them in light of my current knowledge and growth. I could choose to put them back on the shelf, along with my other limiting beliefs and character defects I had retired. I did not have to place my belief in ideas that were not aligned with the positive experiences in my life. The intuitive thoughts and insights that I received were God's way of *"removing"* what was so troubling for me. This process and result has been true in every area of my life.

This process *always* begins with my admission of needing help with the force of habit. I cannot remove my own shortcomings without some kind of outside help, and decided that I did not want to live that way anymore. This process also involves preparation to grieve for what you are about to outgrow. Preparation and humility are required, prior to asking your Higher Power in Step Seven, to remove your shortcomings from you.

PREPARATION AND HUMILITY

It is human nature to resist letting go of core habits, however dysfunctional they might be. It is also human, and part of every survivor's journey into recovery, to feel misgivings, doubts, and even trepidation, when considering the absence of character defects that have been in operation all of your life. Perhaps these defects even saved your life. You needed them to survive; to get by in the world, when you had no other knowledge or functional tools for how to make it in this often lonely and confusing journey. Some survivors spend a lifetime maintaining a certain story about them; only to discover through taking the steps, that their story contains myths that are in conflict with spiritual principles (and especially with the truth). Your whole self-image may need to be re-examined, as you prepare yourself with humility to evaluate what is no longer serving you.

Even though you have taken Steps Four and Five, you may not be totally clear as to the difference between your *character,* and your *character defects.* The field of mental health will inform you that a person's personality is a complex structure, and if you get caught up in trying to figure out exactly why, where, when, or how you got to be the way you are, you can fall into the trap of self-obsession and self-absorption. The goal of Step Six is to have **clarity and self-awareness** of your shortcomings, so that you can become **entirely ready** for the God of your understanding to remove them. The goal is NOT to indulge in regret or in self-obsession. The goal is to make a reasonable effort to understand which character defects are you inner roadblocks, develop insight into your particular character, and to pray for their removal.

The wisdom and effectiveness of Step Six can be seen in *The Transtheoretical Model of Behavior Change,* the work of Prochaska, J.O. and DiClemente, C.C. This highly popular model evaluates and documents a person's readiness to act on a new, healthier behavior. As with anything that requires appropriate preparation, changing unhealthy behavioral patterns is no different.

Preparation and humility *are* compatible with each other, but without a working definition of humility, these two can seem like opposite attitudes. Genuine humility comes from a sense of power. However, it is not the kind of power that comes from a demanding ego, aggression, or power struggle. It is also not about a shamefaced attitude or self-deprecation. Rather, humility is intimate knowledge of your genuine self: your gifts, strengths, needs, and limitations. It also includes a felt experience that there is a "Higher Presence" in the world, and that you are not an island on to yourself. To assist you right now in having such a felt experience, imagine that you were invited to dinner with that one person you feel is most untouchable; someone you were very much in awe of. Unless you are a narcissist, you most likely will feel empowered and rejuvenated by such an encounter. Preparing yourself to *"have God remove all these defects of character"*, at minimum, must involve sensing this Presence. Sensing this presence can be life altering, and I would encourage you to become absorbed with this experience through prayer and meditation.

Character defects gradually have less power in your life as you focus on its opposite trait, and maintain a regular spiritual discipline. If you are willing to surrender, you have become *entirely ready* to stop letting go of both holding on and of withholding. Every character defect is in essence, a holding on and a withholding. When you let it go (stop using the same broken tools), you invite your Higher Power to do for you what you could not do alone.

Humility is a powerful motivator in thoroughly evaluating your approach to getting your needs met; and answering these questions may bring you some clarity on this matter. However, take caution to do this writing exercise with a compassionate frame-of-mind. After all, it is hard to see how you stay stuck in old programming, if you are using a familiar but unkind attitude of harshness, rage, self-rejection, or judgment towards yourself.

1) What are my top five character defects, and in what ways do I rely on them in order to get my needs met?

_____

_____

_____

_____

2) What effect does acting on these character defects have on myself and on other people?

_____

_____

Trauma and Transformation: A 12-Step Guide.

_____

_____

3) Why do I clutch on to this pattern?

_____

_____

_____

_____

4) What real of imagine threat do I face if I gave this pattern up?

_____

_____

_____

_____

5) Do I honestly believe my Higher Power is greater than my defects, and can support me as I take this emotional risk?

_____

_____

_____

_____

6) What spiritual principle can I apply to this process? (Examples include: commitment, courage, trust, self-honesty, faith, kindness, willingness, perseverance, love, forgiveness, understanding, compassion, humor, and patience).

_____

_____

_____

_____

In order to unlock yourself from old patterns of behaving and relating to other people, you need to unclench your fists and start from where you are. This calls for prayer and patience. I would also encourage you to keep a journal to record your thoughts, feelings, moods, dreams, insights, and ideas. Keeping a journal is analogous to taking a photo of what is going on inside you. Preparation is non-negotiable when you are doing an inside job; because it is the beginning of transforming your trauma.

If you are one of those survivors who struggles with fear, and this fear is preventing you from moving forward, remember that fear gradually disappears when you turn on the light. As an analogy, your relationship to your fears can be compared to how a shadow boxer relates to their shadow. A shadow boxer sees their own shadow, but sees this image as another, real person. They box with their own shadow relentlessly, using all their might and fury; when in reality there is no one there, but themselves.

You can apply trust to this process; take action to turn on the light, and use your awareness to see that *fear is sometimes a*

false alarm. Using a common childhood fear of monsters in the closet, you can be the responsible and comforting adult who turns on the closet light so the child will see that there are no monsters hiding out. However, aspects of this work are solitary events.

You must decide if you will finally challenge your fears. No matter what you find in your inner closets, deliberately choose to turn on the light of wisdom and grace. As you take the responsible and comforting action, you may discover that your fears are only your personal shadows of events from long ago.

You may see that the "monster" is all the things you think are beyond redemption in you. The "monster" can also be understood as your "shadow side". According to Carl Gustav Jung, it is the embodiment of everything in you which you do not want to own or acknowledge. The shadow also contains your best talents that could not safely be expressed in the past. Facing yourself with the light on (readiness, humility and prayer), is the essence of Step Six.

WILLINGNESS - NOT A DEMAND FOR PERFECTION

What I personally experienced in this step was a *willingness to let go of my "trauma-reactive" habits, and not a self-demand to be perfect.* This willingness helped me to be aware *when I was falling back into old patterns of thinking and behaving.* I also developed an appreciation that even if no one knows that I am acting based on a character defect that acting out is still an injury to my spiritual growth. My spiritual growth has become so important to me, because I discovered its relationship to the amount of joy and peace that I feel inside.

The willingness that Step Six calls for, involves trust and faith that my Higher Power will continue to work in my life exactly as I need it. For example, I trust that my Higher Power will not remove my defect of emotional dishonesty to make me into a brutally honest person, who is not capable of remaining silent, even if my words of truth will hurt someone. I find that as I become genuinely open to taking responsibility for applying spiritual principles, I am most likely not going to fall into the same old traps. I am a human being, with flaws, imperfections, assets, gifts, talents, and human needs. I am never going to become perfect – not in the next twenty-four hours, not ever. With this attitude, my understanding of myself and vision for my life is far more hopeful and positive. Willingness to change, and not a demand for perfection, which takes place in Steps Six and Seven, provides the groundwork to make amends in Steps Eight and Nine. Without this willingness to change, there is no use to make amends.

Take a moment now to examine some of your own trauma-reactive habits, as evidenced by your personal cycles of relationships. For example, if you are a "rescuer/fixer" (co-dependent) your motivation is to "fix" the other person, based on what *you* think is correct for them, but you neglect your own needs and feelings. This is a very common survival mechanism employed by trauma survivors. The truly loving way to relate to people is to afford them the dignity of their own process.

Another common survival mechanism is excessive people-pleasing. People who have this trait are lacking healthy emotional boundaries. They struggle with *"saying no when I mean no, and saying yes when I mean yes"*. In response to their way of relating to people, the **Fixers and Rescuers** feel a chronic and draining sense of dominant failure, pain, and toxic attachment to people who will join them in such a heartbreaking repetitive cycle.

THREE QUESTIONS FOR REFLECTION

1) Have you found that it is much easier for you to give in to others, rather than express what *you need and want*?

_____

_____

_____

_____

2) Have you used this character defect as a form of control, manipulation, or avoidance?

_____

_____

_____

_____

3) Are you willing, right now, to have these character defects removed by your Higher Power?

_____

_____

_____

_____

For some of you, your main character defect may be a life-long presentation as **The Perpetual Victim. Victims** usually get themselves into trouble, and then make someone, other than themselves, responsible for their behavior. They rarely follow through with getting help, and complain a lot when they tell their story. Such people attract **Fixers and Rescuers**. Victims end up shaming their fixers and rescuers by conveying that did not get the help they are entitled to, and somehow it was their fault. They rage at this failure; their demand was not met! Some other examples of character defects include: Perfectionism, Failures, Martyrs,

Addicts, Grandiosity, Narcissism, Selfishness, Bullies, Abusers, and Chronic Comedians.

Are you now wondering if such survival mechanisms, which, after all, helped you to survive, will be that easy to simply "let go" – even if you are "entirely ready"? Do you identify with any of this? If yes, using your favorite role/character defect that you take on when relating to people, answer the following:

Trauma and Transformation: A 12-Step Guide.

My Role/Character Defect that I take on in relationships	Who or what is reinforcing this role? (Ex: unacceptable wishes, fantasies, anxiety, career choice, family relationships, etc).	What is the magical quality of this role? (Ex: relieves my anxiety, symbolizes the only way to have value, and keeps the danger away).	What is the emotional danger in exploring, and maybe letting go of this role, in favor of being true to you? Are you overestimating the danger involved?	How can your increased understanding allow you to meet your needs for closeness, distance, and independence in a loving, safe way?

Let us look at the character defect of *selfishness*. Suffice it to say that many a person has struggled with this, and sought for it to be removed. Selfishness is an example of a deeply ingrained pattern of relating to people (clinically referred to as 'Object Relations'), that does not leave you so easily. And by default, selfish people may not have any awareness, nor be bothered that they are selfish.

Estan is an example of a classically selfish person, whom I agreed to assist as he journeyed through the Twelve Steps. When he came to Step Six, he knew selfishness was an issue for him because he had heard it often from others in his life. He felt that preparing himself to not be selfish, was impossible. I suggested that he draw three lists, labeled as follows: 1) *"Character Defects that I am ready to let go of* **now**". 2) *"Not now, but* **maybe someday** *I will let go of this trait"*. 3) *"My Character* **Strengths** *that can help me to*

Trauma and Transformation: A 12-Step Guide.

overcome my character defects. (In social work, this is referred to as "*The Strengths Perspective*").

Character Defects that I am ready to let go of **now.**	Not now, but maybe someday I will let go of this trait.	My Character Strengths that can help me to overcome my character defects.

Estan agreed to continue with the rest of his step work, but found himself bothered by his lack of honesty. *"How can I continue taking the steps, while I avoid the biggest piece to my own puzzle?"* Estan stated that compulsive selfishness, one of his most dominant character defects, and the root cause of his relationship problems, can no longer go unchecked. He wanted to change, and believed that he could. He acknowledged that without taking Step Six, he would continue to have significant difficulties. However, the idea of not living from a self-centered, selfish platform terrified and angered him. He felt chronically entitled, and believed he was "owed" by anyone who got into a relationship with him. This *"cognitive dissonance"*, a feeling of discomfort when you have two inconsistent beliefs about the same issue, troubled him greatly. I pointed that this is his powerlessness on display. He saw that he had minimal control over this character trait, and that it ruled his life in a destructive way. The preparedness to change came out of his volition to solve the puzzle of his unhappy life. He became willing and ready to take on this issue.

As we continued our exploration together, Estan learned of his reasons for not wanting to part with his selfish behavior. His mother was a narcissist and never showed empathy, or genuine interest, in him. His father was completely unavailable emotionally, spending long periods away from him. Estan's early childhood was marked by loneliness, feeling ignored, a sense of alienation, and a general experience of being unwanted by his parents.

Sadly for this little boy, life revolved around his narcissistic mother. There was no healthy mirroring from either of his parents or any genuine, consistent connection to Estan. Developmentally, he did not have the loving parenting to enable him to identify how he felt, what he believed in, or what he needed. These basic questions that a functional adult would ask eluded him. The relationship with his mother continued to be a troubled one. Estan describes this experience as: *"traumatic to the little boy I once was"*. To ease his isolation and suffering, Estan had created an alternate reality in his mind. He imagined that he was the king of a huge castle, and had everyone and everything at his disposal. He spent many hours alone fantasizing about being worshipped, valued, admired, and in control. This became so real to him that often times Estan 'forgot' who he really was: a suffering, neglected, and deeply lonely child.

I pointed out that his use of imagination was his main defense in coping with such an unbearable home life. His imagination and fantasies gave him the yearned-for sensation that he was powerful, in control, and adored instead of isolated, powerless, and neglected.

He felt baffled at the notion that "*my childhood imagination created a way of relating to people that brings me so much pain*". And indeed, you hold on to behaviors, patterns, and traits that cause you the most suffering and problems. How illogical! But anyone with deeply rooted survival defenses, unconsciously choose those patterns that will most enable them to remain separate from their pain.

Fortunately for you, Estan and other survivors, you grow stronger and more secure when you follow a spiritually sound plan to transform your wounds into wisdom. Eventually you develop the necessary ego strength so that your age-old defenses are not as necessary. In Twelve Step programs, following a spiritual path of the Twelve Steps is done with a recovery support network. If you are not in a Twelve Step program, I strongly recommend that you either share with your existing support network (if it is safe and growth oriented), or develop one.

Let us return to Estan's process. When the first opportunity came up for him to revert to his selfish behavior, he immediately gave me a call, as I had invited him to do. Estan's neighbor, Abigail, requested that he lend her $400 for basic necessities. In the past, Estan would have lent it to her, but at a steep price. He would have expected her to babysit at a whim, and if she would say no, he would get hostile and angry, and remind her of his favors: "*...even though I didn't really want to help you, I knew you were desperate so I gave in*". Of course this was highly painful for Abigail, who felt too weak and needy to confront him. He acknowledged that he hurt her and, in fact, relished the power he had over her.

I asked Estan to pause and reflect on his motives before lending her the money. Can he honestly lend it to her with no demands, or mean words exchanged, except to have the $400 returned as per their agreement? He confessed that he could not, because his selfish and controlling urge felt too intense for him. I suggested that lending Abigail the money would then be a bribe, and not an honest loan. After consideration, he chose not to lend it to her. Since this was the first time Estan refused her request to borrow money, to his surprise, she did not react well to it. Estan described his reaction as feeling *"insecure and knocked off my beam"*. This is very typical when you stop reacting in familiar ways, and take the emotional risk to try something healthier. The fear of stepping into the unknown is something that trauma survivors are intimately familiar with. It is also a fear that is healed through prayer, practice, patience, and compassion.

Estan reports being dedicated to his personal spiritual growth, and feeling less strapped down by his old, familiar ways. He grew in strength, and stated *"that change is not as scary as I thought it would be". I almost regret not having worked on myself sooner. I would have spared many a person, mostly myself, a lot of suffering"*. He got in the habit of pausing and reflecting on his true motivations, and then acting in accordance with good, orderly direction (G.O.D). He refers to this effort *"as a daily reprieve that I earn because as I learn better, I do better"*. He learned and practiced how to give genuinely. His most prized payoff has become a serene conscience. How about you? What is your most prized, non-tangible reward? Using the sample charts below, identify what you are willing to let go of *right now*, to facilitate a Golden Exchange.

The Serene Conscience – an Exercise in a Golden Exchange

What I am willing to let go of right now...	In exchange for...
Unfairly blaming or idealizing other people	Compassion and genuine warmth.
Denial of reality	Courage, truthfulness, taking emotional risks to face what is in front of you
Becoming whatever someone else wants you to be, even if you have to go against yourself.	Creating a safe holding environment, so you develop your own identify, and are real with yourself and others
Refuse to cooperate, are negative, put others down, or are grandiose (condescending)	Genuine closeness with others, respect, open-mindedness, selflessness.
Aggressive and hostile towards yourself or others.	Gentleness, kindness, fairness, love, sensitivity.

Trauma and Transformation: A 12-Step Guide.

YOUR' Serene Conscience – What is your Golden Exchange?

What I am willing to let go of right now...	In exchange for...

Some trauma survivors have a tendency towards a path of drama. One common explanation for this, which originated with Freud, is that people who have been wounded usually repress and suppress the feelings that once needed full expression. The drama and its stage serve the purpose of telling the story, where there are no adequate words or conscious memories for resolving it. Drama also prevents people from revealing what they are really feeling and/or experiencing in life. Drama keeps old defenses alive and well. And all this equally maintains survivors in a self-absorbed existence instead of meaningful self-awareness.

Take a moment now to say the following prayer, meditate on the words, and write your reactions below.

"Higher Power, I give you this defect of *(egotism, envy, pride, fear, guilt, resentment, Jealousy, gluttony, dishonesty, sloth, rage, selfishness, self-pity, arrogance, grandiosity, etc)*, **and I ask you to remove it from me, by opening my mind and heart to a new way of being. AMEN."**

_____

_____

_____

_____

With every sincere prayer, I gained a certain clarity and perspective that was not there before. I did not think it could be that simple. **Simple prayer, with the intent just to communicate with God is all that is required here.** The more I practiced this approach, the more aware I became that I have a loving, personal Higher Power. It also helped me with affect regulation, since prayer is a powerful form of intimate expression, release, and connection. To my delight,

I developed increased trust and an appreciation for simplicity, as I applied this step consistently to my difficult experiences.

Simplicity and trust are by-products of an ongoing process of reaching out to my Higher Power. Initially, I never thought that trust in my Creator was even possible for me to genuinely experience. I was also not interested in developing this spiritual relationship, because my psychic schema had trust chained to acute betrayal-pain. However, overcoming my conflict with Step Six was the beginning of a more enlightened perspective on remaining open and courageous to face my deepest obstacles. This experience granted me a clear vision that is unique for me. I began the process of letting go of what was useless to me, and embracing what was meaningful and powerful in my life. And slowly, I observed my own strength develop: spiritually, mentally, and emotionally.

AWARENESS IS NOT ENOUGH ON ITS OWN

Awareness is powerful, but not enough as a standalone. Without targeted action, you will not move yourself forward. Seeing what you have long- avoided can be hard to digest, and knowing exactly what right action to take can be confusing. For example, let's assume that you were raised in a family where you were never taught any healthy forms of communication, emotional language, appropriate boundaries, and were traumatized. You may have the body and functioning of an adult, but go through life functioning emotionally as the wounded child you once may have been. This is why developing spiritually sound self-esteem (not feeling unworthy or inadequate, accepting your strengths and weakness, feel good, capable and loved) is so critical to growing up emotionally.

It is natural for children to exhibit self-centeredness because that is age-appropriate, part of being a child. When certain character defects persist into adulthood, they are a symptom of emotional immaturity and imbalance. These childhood qualities belong on the list of Step Six. Identifying these character defects initiates the process of change. This list can get you started: chronic people-pleasing, approval-seeking, inappropriate dependency on others, or extreme independency, having "walls" instead of safe boundaries, or being without any boundaries at all, compulsive jealousy, laziness, dishonesty, or passive-aggressive responses. Make a list of those character defects that you feel cause you the most imbalance in your life.

This is my favorite analogy for understanding both awareness and lack of awareness. I am walking around in a dark room, constantly bumping into the furniture and other obstacles. I get all banged up, trip, fall flat on my face, and end up injured and confused. I stumble upon the lamp, turn it on, and I am relieved by the light. With awareness (the lamp's light) I can clearly see my unhealthy patterns (obstacles in the room). But after a while, I can easily take this light for granted, and simply get used to it. That's human nature. When I become ready to act on my new insight, I begin with preparation. That is the logical order of things. I begin preparing to rearrange the furniture in the room, so I can freely walk here and not hurt myself. Some of the furniture will need to be thrown away. Some I need to re-upholster, and some I just need to re-arrange.

Beth told me of her tendency to rage, attack, and blame other people, while *never* taking any ownership *for her part of a conflict or problem.* She never questioned herself: *"How did **I** get the ball rolling in this situation?"* Working on Step Six, she recalled that as an adolescent she was frequently attacked by her parents for minor infractions. As a protective defense, and without any other healthy coping mechanisms, she began screaming and blaming her parents during each incident. She desperately did not want to feel so attacked, ashamed, and defeated. She carried this behavior on to all of her adult relationships, which was not serving her well at all. She knew how frightened and uncomfortable people were around her, like she felt around her parents, but not responding this way, to her, meant to open herself to attack. As a result of her persistent and genuine step work, she decided to not respond to a provocation without counting to ten inwardly, no matter how tempted she was to conduct a shame/rage attack on the other person. She tried this for a week and then compulsively exploded in rage towards a loved one. She expressed her regret and pain in the following way: *"I took a step through the gates of my own hell and couldn't see past the smoke and fire to get out"*. I encouraged her to keep a log of her attempts, and start over, beginning right now. She felt motivated enough to follow my suggestion.

Perhaps you can identify with Beth, and have stepped over your inner threshold, only to find yourself passing through to the gates of your own hell, by repeating painful patterns you swore off. These are the exact patterns or defects that belong on your Sixth Step list. People who *react* instead of *respond* are in most need to have God "remove such defects", as it is usually out of impulsivity (without thought) and historical (it reminds you of something else, not necessarily based on what is going on right now).

If you can identify your personal stuck points, you can devise and pursue a plan to retire them. Having awareness (knowing which broken tool you can trade in for an upgraded, functional tool), coupled with humility (realistic acceptance), will make it easier for you to trust in your Higher Power. Remain open-minded (consider both sides to the matter) that each difficult (but not dangerous) moment is an opportunity to replace your most troubling defects go.

KEEP IT MOVING FORWARD

A very common and favorite saying in the Twelve Step rooms is the following: "**We claim spiritual progress rather than spiritual perfection.**" The golden key is to remain honest actively involved in your change-process. At times you may feel unwilling, too imperfect, or just uninspired. It is also natural to question, with a pang of pain, why the people who have perpetrated the trauma are not doing the work instead of you. Shouldn't you be deemed innocent of this whole process?! I, like countless others, have felt this way, and it makes perfect sense. But then I realized that even if I adapted to my situation with the help of these character defects, they are no longer necessary.

I became "entirely ready" to examine their role in my life, and ask for God to remove them. I concluded that I am responsible for *my* choice to take the steps, so as not to be lured into familiar patterns that cause me futile pain. This is where the power of willingness and humility come in. I do not believe anyone can be forced into genuine willingness. If you are not willing, accept that this is how it is right now.

If you are having a hard time with being willing to look at your character defects and have God help you with them, you may want to explore some of the possible underlying reasons for this. There are many trauma survivors who have never adequately processed their pain and grief. Their mind shielded itself by repressing and suppressing the core pain, feelings and memories associated with their worst suffering. Repression can manifest as addictive behaviors, compulsions, and various psychiatric disorders. If you had to deny what happened, and keep shameful secrets buried deeply under tight lock and key, most likely you are harboring distortions: spiritually, emotionally, sexually, physically, and mentally. ***It is to your benefit to connect with your Higher Power on***

this intimate level. Bring your broken heart to God, just as a child innocently brings their broken toy for their trustworthy parent to fix.

Some trauma survivors have a tendency to strive for perfection, and some always look for loop holes and various distractions to avoid fulfilling their responsibilities. When you take Step Six, you turn on the light of awareness so you can identify your character defects, and prepare to have God **remove them all**. This is not a magical process and you do not need to be "worthy" to ask for this removal. Just prepare yourself to humbly ask. It is your chance to prepare for a partnership with your Higher Power, so that the next step in your transformation from trauma can take place.

Sometimes your Higher Power will choose to "remove" character defects which are not on your list. This can manifest as "sublimation", which according to Freud, means that you channel your character defects to its opposite. So instead of a literal removal by God, they are transformed into character strength - or you simply lose your compulsion to act them out.

REVIEW AND MOVING ON

It is common for survivors of trauma to feel that their spirit is undernourished, and saddled with many moments of regret and shame. Perhaps you long for a past so different, so that you would not carry the troublesome baggage containing character defects, fears, insecurities, pain, addictions, or compulsions. You may linger in the resentment that life blocked you from experiencing emotional freedom, or the fulfillment of your dreams. Perhaps you do not believe that you are actually capable of rising above your deepest challenges.

You have to begin your growth somewhere, and it is usually with questions that are painful, and seem to have no answers. As you take Step Six, you will enhance the vision of the life you are living, by clearly seeing how much freer you can be without blockage from your character defects and inner conflicts.

WRITING EXERCISE

Take time now to write a vision of yourself with the qualities you are seeking. The purpose for having a clear and goal-directed vision is to have a personal springboard into the next step, Step Seven. Step Seven is about humbly asking God to remove your shortcomings, so you need to make sure that you have a clear idea of what they are, why you want them removed, and if you have the humility to make this request.

Trauma and Transformation: A 12-Step Guide.

1. What will my life look like?

_____

_____

_____

_____

2. Will my life inspire myself and others?

_____

_____

_____

_____

3. Will my willingness give me the strength to move into a graceful spiritual expression of myself?

_____

_____

_____

_____

Write your immediate reaction to the following sentence, including emotions, thoughts, and bodily sensations:

"I, (write your full name here) have always been beautiful and valuable since the day God created me. But certain things happened to me, and my beauty and value has been covered up. I am now capable of discarding what is no longer useful in me, so I can live a life that is a true expression of the Real Me".

_____

_____

_____

_____

STEP SEVEN

Humbly asked Him to remove our shortcomings.

Step Seven is about humility (realistic, selfless, and modest) and *asking* for help to make the changes you are now prepared for. Consider Step Seven as a portal into openness for change. Once you take Step Seven, you step out of the way so your Higher Power can handle the rest of it. The combination of *humility* and *asking* provides a survivor with a perspective beyond the traumatic events. Sadly, you can form an inaccurate perspective based on how you internalized the traumatic event(s). Through prayer (humbly asking), you can trust that your prayers are heard, shall be answered in God's time only.

Some common questions from survivors before taking Step Seven may include: *"Will my part be good enough? Will I be ready (conscious) enough so that my Higher Power can help me? What if I think I am ready, but on an unconscious level, I am not? Will doing my part actually work? Will my Higher Power show up for me the way I need it? What if this Step does not actually work? What if my prayer is not as sincere as it should be?"* In its most simple and pure form, asking for help (praying) is a partnership agreement with your Creator. One of my favorite quotes about prayer, is *"Prayer is asking, and meditation is listening"*. I remind you that if you were able to do this on your own, you would simply do it and get on with life. **But by the time you seek spiritual guidance you have acknowledged that a Super Power is needed for this venture.** If you have been thoroughly honest with your process thus far, you will identify those traits, inner conflicts, and distortions that require a Super Power's intervention.

There are concrete benefits of allowing a Super Power to help your transformation process. For one, your self-image will shift depending on how you understand yourself in relation to the God of your understanding. If you have ever assumed that God does not love you, or want to be there for you, what does this reveal about your self-worth? If you were shunned by your caregivers, your personalized replica of how God relates to you would be a distance and cold relationship, or not one at all. Your need for a connected, intimate, spiritual love with your Higher Power is equal to the need you had for such a relationship with your caregivers. Your relationship with the God of your understanding is another manifestation of your internalized "Object Relations" (your way of relating to people that was shaped when you were an infant). With this perspective, you may find yourself more interested and open to learning about love and of the connection that flows from *"humbly asked..."*

If it appears that you are not in charge of when your life will change, or that it does not follow your personal agenda, take note that this is a fundamental reality of practicing humility.

Whether you pray for change for the internal or external aspects of your life, you do not stand in full control of this process. The good news is that as long as you cooperate with Divine Intelligence, doing your best to remain humble, conscious, and honest, you allow for Grace to enter your process.

A CHILD'S HUMILITY – A LESSON IN ASKING FOR HELP

I want you to take a moment now, and imagine a five year old girl, Carole, asking her parents for help to overcome her tendency to bully other kids over toys. She asks her parents in a direct and sincere way - the way that children communicate. That is the purest form of humility. Her parents are delighted that she has the sense to know right from wrong, wants to amend her behavior, AND feels loved enough to ask them for help. This is part of their joy in parenting. The same reaction is experienced by your Higher

Power when you take Step Seven. You can never go wrong in coming from this part of yourself when you humbly ask God for help.

Survivors may react when they see the word *"humbly"* in this step. Some traumatic experiences include feeling low, diminished, silenced, and demeaned in a significant way. The word "humble", without the correct definition, can bring you back to a time and place when you were undervalued, demeaned or made to feel inferior. If you grew up in an abusive environment, your needs were not welcome. It is easy to mistake Step Seven as a step of passivity, the time to apologize for inner struggles, wants or needs. As an example, Little Carole can teach you about true humility. **She has a strong sense of who she is as she asks her parents for help.** Although she does not know what the results of her request will be, she has a basic sense of trust in her parents, and is content with simply asking.

You are the child of an Almighty Creator, who views you with the same love, tenderness and joy as Carole's parents when she asks them for help. **If you can imagine this, you have completed Step Seven**. Even if you believe that you are "damaged" as a result of what you survived, you are not incapable of humbly asking for help. I urge you not to let your sense of "brokenness" stop you from asking your Higher Power for help to heal, grow, and live out your potential to the fullest extent possible. **True humility is about being grounded in your Higher Power's version of your truth and self-worth**.

If you have inaccurate self-esteem, and find yourself connecting humility with being unworthy, I suggest that you imagine what your Creator thinks of you. You have been handcrafted: deliberately, patiently, lovingly, and with great accuracy in the exact likeliness of your Creator. This Creator is against any form of abuse, and any perpetration by humans against each other, animals or the planet. So by taking Step Seven, you are choosing to align yourself with this Captain. Alternatively, you can align yourself with the other side, and believe all the falsehoods that are attached to trauma caused by human perpetration.

STREAM-OF-CONSCIOUS WRITING EXERCISE TO GET THE RELATIONSHIP RIGHT

Using your dominant hand, write the following question at least 5 times below: *God, what do you really think of me?*	Using your NON-dominant hand, answer in the way that a most loving, intimately-connected God would answer you.

What was your experience doing this exercise? Do you like the idea of a loving God responding to you, but still harbor serious doubts or fears about this relationship? Many survivors have a shattered sense of meaning and cannot fathom a sense of coherence in a benign universe. However, if you give yourself a choice: either God CAN, or CANNOT help you, what choice do you have here? I prefer to believe that God CAN help me, and that is my starting point. I acknowledge that I am responsible for my life.

However, I am not in complete control of my life. This is self-empowering humility, because I do not have to do it all. I only have to do my part, with all of my strengths and limitations. As long as I proceed with honesty I can rest assured that I have done my part sufficiently. Doing my part especially includes taking credit when I do the right thing, overcome a negative habit, or tell the truth when I least want to.

Asking for help from a benign universe may create a feeling inside of you that you are part of something greater than you. Establishing this as your response to crises, especially if you feel your faith is in crises, may provide you with a significant psychological benefit. There are different forms of asking, and to gain clarity with the words "humbly asking", take a moment now to self-define both *"humbly asking"*, and just *"asking"*. What have you discovered?

Self-define: "humbly asking".	Self-define: "asking".

When I pray with humility, I acknowledge that God is not my "Gal Friday" or errand-boy. I do not submit a list of demands or requests, and expect them to be done on *my* time. You can take a look in society, and see clearly that humility is not a very popular trait. You live in a world driven by supply and demand, the need for increased power, prestige, and materialistic acquisition. There seems to be little mention or need for humility. This word is often associated with weakness and can invite ridicule or abuse. It is not a concept that society rewards. If you are not comfortable with this word, how then will you be free to ask God in this fashion? Answer this question below.

_____

_____

_____

_____

When you "humbly ask", versus just 'asking', you stand at your true height, in partnership with something much greater than yourself. Humbly asking also involves asking without pride, without the sense that everything is dependent only on the Great Big I Am (egocentric thinking). The opposite of humility is arrogant pride, the hallmark of a weak ego. When you ask with the absence of humility, this pride has free reign and the asking is actually *demanding*. When you arrogantly demand from God, or anyone else, what are the consequences? Using your personal experiences, fill out the table below.

The time I arrogantly demanded	The consequence	The time I humbly asked	The consequence

P.R.A.Y.E.R = Powerful **R**elease **A**lways **Y**ours **E**verywhere **R**egardless.

What else should a survivor pray for, in addition to removal of shortcomings? Pray for an increased *sense of compassion and understanding* for the suffering you went through. Pray for an in-depth understanding of healing and spirituality. Pray for the willingness to see the right healers, and to have a receptive dialogue with him/her. Pray for a commitment to your overall health, and that you do not make addictions, compulsions, or chronic avoidance your solution to your pain. Pray for the spiritual guidance to tell your story in a way that creates healing, effective solutions, and inspiration for others. Pray for the knowledge of God's will for you, and the motivation to carry it out. This always includes joy, abundance and well-being.

My friend Rebecca prefers to say the Serenity Prayer when she practices Step Seven. The Serenity Prayer has helped an untold number of people to stop wrestling with people, places, things, thoughts, feelings, beliefs, and character traits (our own and others).

> *God grant me the serenity*
> *To accept the things I cannot change,*
> *Courage to change the things I can*
> *And wisdom to know the difference.* [6]

A popular suggestion often utilized in the Twelve Step meeting rooms for externalizing Step Seven is to create a "*God-Box*". I personally love ceremonies and rituals, because rituals make things real and immediate, and I took to this suggestion immediately. I took a nice-size shoe box and fully

---

[6] *Twelve Steps and Twelve Traditions*, New York: Alcoholics Anonymous World Services, Inc., 1981. (The "Twelve and Twelve.") Pg. 41

decorated it. On the outside of it I labeled it "*My personal God-Box*", and in meditative fashion, I placed small, handwritten personal struggles that I was eager for my Higher Power to remove from me. This was my way of symbolizing that I was entirely ready, right now, to give them up.

I decided that once I dropped the pieces of paper in this box, the matter is now strictly in my Higher Power's care. Anytime I wished to take my control back, I can simply take that note out of the box. It has been years since I have created my God-box, and to date, I have never taken anything out of it. I keep it where I can see it several times a day, as a reassurance that I never have to pick up the pattern, person, problem, or issue again. I believe (and not feel because feelings change all the time, and belief is consistent and runs very deep) that God's will for me is for love, connection and abundant joy. Not the chronic pain and misunderstandings I was clutching on to.

I encourage you to be creative and devise your own method to accomplish the spiritual practice of *asking for help* and then *letting go of the results*. Use any other creative process that is personally helpful. As long as you are accountable and responsible for your behavior, you will receive the help that you ask for. As you become more familiar with this process and way of responding, you will begin to understand that by asking and surrendering, you strengthen your ability to make choices and to remain accountable. If you stop practicing your character defects, and you ask God to help you remove them, you have a recipe for success!

To illustrate this point, let us take a look at Richard. Richard's highest priority was getting rid of excessive caretaking in relationships. He began to question if his behavior had any manipulative aspects to it, because his underlying fear is that he is not lovable unless he extends himself excessively and with little reciprocity. So his "love" covered up his shameful secret: that he was inherently not lovable or good enough just as he was. He also stated that while friends claim that he is a loyal friend, he makes little effort to let them in equally. He has a tendency to get too involved in their lives, excessively distressing about their needs and circumstances. This leaves him with little time, energy, or interest to care for his own needs and growth. I pointed out to Richard, that with the proper guidance, he can channel his abundance energy and empathy for others into taking better care of himself. Often times, people who are codependent, are sending a message of how *they themselves* want to be treated, but in fact, are deprived. They are acting out their deepest, unfulfilled need. If Richard's experience resonates with you, you may want to further examine this issue in your life. As you begin practicing how to take better care for yourself, you may not feel so compelled to focus on others.

Ben's issues are similar to Richard's issues. Ben acknowledged that he finds himself paralyzed by his need to be perfect. He feels anxiety almost all of the time, because he believes that everything has to be done in the "perfect way". He understands that he developed perfectionism because his father, in drunken episodes, would viciously accuse and criticize him harshly. In order to manage his terror and anxiety, Ben was constantly focused on making everything perfect. He hoped his father would notice, which he never did. Ben says that he is far from living his potential, because he worries so much about what other people will think of him. He is afraid that if he is imperfect, others will not approve of him, and this was unbearably terrifying for him. Ben describes this as *"my personal obsession with perfection"*, and attributes it to a deep depression and a cycle of feelings of "*going mad*". I advised Ben, that before he totally gives up his perfectionism (another common result of trauma and neglect), he may actually have some hidden treasures in this pattern.

When we reviewed his strengths and weaknesses, we discovered his attention to details, accuracy and concern for his work. I explained that if he has the willingness to be released from the grips of perfectionism, he can fully enjoy the fruits of his labor. Ben was able to agree with me on this point. I also reminded him that he has received acknowledgement in his professional career for his aspiration for quality and excellence which has brought him financial rewards, as well. He hesitated to admit that his friends and colleagues have praised him for paying attention to details about them that others have not noticed.

Ben was able to re-frame what he thought was "my greatest weakness and tormentor" into a commitment to treating himself with the attention and quality of care he extends to others. He was able to see a painful pattern **as simply falling short of his potential**. This removed the heavy weight of self-blame, sense of defeat and failure. He simply had to ask himself: "how can my perfectionist pattern work *for me*?"

Ben learned a paradox while taking Step Seven: if I can accept myself *just as I am*, I have a pretty good chance I *can* change. He still lapses into self-criticism, but stops himself as soon as he notices his fault-finding and perfectionist pattern repeat itself. He understands its origins, and is learning to cooperate with his Higher Power to replace this wound-based approach. He discovered the relief of compassion and self-acceptance, which helped him prepare for Step Eight.

LET'S GO TREASURE HUNTING! AN EXERCISE IN SEEKING THE GOLD IN YOUR CHARACTER FLAWS

In the following exercise, you will seek to identify several of your heavy weight character defects that give you the greatest sense of self-defeat or failure. See if you can find the hidden treasure in this pattern, and how you can channel it in a healthy, constructive way. Once you find the treasure, **do not** use it as a justification for continued use of this heavy-weight defect, but as a motivator to make good use of it, as you map out your ongoing journey.

My heavy-weight character defect that gives me the greatest sense of self-defeat or failure.	I found the Treasure! This is how I can channel it in a healthy, constructive way.

PRIDE AND ITS INTERFERENCE WITH SPIRITUAL COOPERATION

When you cooperate with humility, you set aside your pride. With this state of mind, you can examine what is really important for you in life, and how your values manifest in relation to others. When your pride is running the show, and you ask for whatever it is you want, pride substitutes for a higher power. With pride, you will not be asking questions such as:

1) Are you being helpful in life, and part of the solution?

_____

_____

_____

_____

2) Do you value spirituality, and how do you display this?

_____

_____

_____

_____

3) How is the God of your understanding operating in your life, and how do you use *this* relationship to make it a better world?

_____

_____

_____

_____

REVIEW AND MOVING ON

When you are trying to live a spiritual program, you want to make sure that there will be nothing as powerful as pride that can work against your efforts to grow spiritually. These questions and your own answers will empower you to live a life of sharing, humility, and remaining proactive in the solution. When you are humble and cooperate, you know that change does not come from a self-centered *will to change*. It is void of the attitude that "*I must do this all by myself, like everything else in my life*". Taking Step Seven is a declaration of a partnership with your Higher Power.

"*Hell is not in torture; Hell is in an empty heart.*" [7]

[7] Gibran, Kahlil. *The Treasured Writings of Kahlil Gibran*, (New York: Castle Books, 2010), Pg. 784.

STEP EIGHT

Made a list of all persons you had harmed, and became willing to make amends to them all.

Step Eight is about unfinished business. This step sets the stage for you to relate to yourself and others in a new way. The first order of business here is to define "harm" and "amends". *Harm* includes the following: damage, impairment, wound, injury, trauma, and change for the worse, any act of sexual abuse, incest, physical injury, and psychological harm, financial or emotional damage. It is the act of spoiling something, or damaging someone.

If you committed harm the way to restore the balance is to make an amends. *Amends* includes a verbal acknowledgement of what was done, *accompanied by a change in behavior*. The change in behavior should mirror the opposite of the harm done. If you are having difficulty identifying what harms you may have done, consider those actions, **or inactions** of yours, that you feel regret for. Since denial can be forceful you may feel you that you are a basically nice person who has not hurt anyone (other than yourself on occasion). If you *suspect* you owe someone an amends, put their name down, and perhaps at a later time, the reason may become clear to you. Any people about whom you feel regret should be placed on your Eighth Step amends list. When you make amends, keep in mind that it is not the normal way of saying "*I am sorry*". It is a commitment to change, and that takes work, especially if you hurt someone due to a general behavioral pattern that you have. The key is to keep an open mind (consider both sides of the matter), because as a helpful saying goes: *"more will be revealed"* if you do.

If you keep yourself open, you will be prepared for what comes when you are ready to face it. Remember, **ALL** human beings are imperfect, and survivors are just as capable of doing harm to themselves or others.

There are harms that cannot be repaired, and those that can be repaired. Examples of harm that cannot be repaired include homicide, property crime (if you cannot compensate your victim), and other violent crimes that result in permanent injury to the person (physical, sexual, spiritual, psychological or emotional harm). Examples of crimes that can be repaired are compensation for harms that have not resulted in permanent damage, being able to provide financial compensation or repairing relationships, to name a few. Since this is a highly personal process, I encourage you to explore what harm you have caused, and if repair is possible. As always, seek honest, wise counsel before proceeding with any decisions or actions.

By the time you reach Step Eight, you will have had some experience in developing a connection with the God of your understanding, and with yourself. This connection is magical bridge between you and others that become involved with your healing process. These are the people that you harmed intentionally, those that you had no desire to hurt but did anyway, those who are not in your life, and those with whom you wish to keep a close, long-term relationship. This is the time when you will discover, identify, and categorize the damage you caused. All the damage you caused goes on this list, and it is irrelevant why you caused the damage. You could have caused it because you were fearful, selfish, entitled, justified, thoughtless, in extreme pain, careless, engulfed with rage, or trying to get your own needs met.

THERE IS NO TIME LIKE THE PRESENT -TAKE STEP EIGHT NOW.

Who or what did I harm or throw off-balance?	What damage did I cause?
MYSELF	

It is generally understood that those who victimize others were once victimized themselves. *In taking this step you seek to <u>not justify</u> causing harm to another person, realizing that such a belief only perpetuates the behavior.* Even if you were harmed in life, *if you have harmed someone*, this principle applies to you unequivocally.

You may really struggle with Step Eight, if there is unprocessed pain because of your traumatic experiences. As you face the challenge of owning your part of doing harm to someone, it may awaken the root of your own pain: **harms done to you**. This can be emotionally consuming, if you are not interested in acknowledging your own pain and suffering. There are survivors who are self-righteous, entitled, and chronically angry. If this describes you, when you get to Step Eight you may have to go back and process your Fourth Step Inventory.

A STRONG WORD OF CAUTION

If you have been victimized by abuse, I ***do not*** suggest you go to your abuser and make amends to your abuser, because you will probably be asking for more abuse. Steps Eight and Nine are applicable to abuse survivors if you have *harmed another person*. If you were abused, your unfinished business can include a deeply rooted ***false*** belief that you are responsible for having been treated that way. If you are unsure about making amends for wrongs you ***did not commit***, please consult with a trusted advisor. Throughout this book, I urge you to consult with such a person during your entire process of the Twelve Steps. You may find it useful to contact Hazelden for their publications of excellent pamphlets and workbooks which provide helpful guidance on working the steps. Examples of appropriate people to share your step work with include a trusted friend, therapist, mentor, or member of the clergy. In Twelve step meetings we say: "*When in doubt – leave it out!*" Obtain objective information so you can see what is really going on with you. ***Please be mindful that if you ask for help from individuals who did not process their own unfinished business in a spiritually sound way, they may devalue and discount the significance of your trauma history.*** In order to heal from trauma, you need a support system of stability, safety, and security. Consulting with the right person is critical to this process, and should never be minimized.

For a trauma survivor taking the Twelve Steps, one of the deepest and most significant understandings is that you are **<u>not</u>** responsible for any childhood neglect and abuse. Taking the steps will help you to see clearly, if this is part of your story, that the harm committed to you was not your fault. You did not deserve the mistreatment, no matter what was told to you to the contrary. Exploring your life through the analytic process of taking the Twelve Steps, may bring out a lot of buried and unknown pain, hurt, conflict and anger. It will also provide you with a constant exercise in telling the truth.

Since you are not responsible for the abuse perpetuated on you in childhood, you need not make any amends to the perpetrators. **If you are currently in a situation where your involvement contributes to your ongoing abuse, seek help immediately. You do not have to live this way, and no one should cause self-harm by remaining loyal to an abuser. There is a lot of good help available. I hope you will strongly consider reaching out for it.**

EMOTIONAL HARMS

Anything that you do that attacks the human heart in a vulnerable place is considered a deep, and damaging harm. Examples include harming another person by manipulation, humiliation, exploitation, neglect, withdrawal, and creating significant fear in them where they believe they are in imminent danger. There are consequences of emotionally harming someone, which include the person(s) experiencing guilt, grief, anger, fear, confusion, and frustration, with the intensity of these emotions varying with the nature of the harm done.

Causing harm to other people also has a huge cost to individuals, communities, and for society-at-large. According to my understanding, humans around the globe have experienced an untold number of assaults, a combination of violent and non-violent crimes. Examples of violent harms involve sexual assault and battery, homicide, physical assault and battery, intimate partner violence, and assault with a deadly weapon. Some examples of non-violent harms involve theft of any kind, or any kind of property damage.

Another impact of harm done to others is the huge burden it places on communities, society-at-large, and on the planet. There are harms done that will wear down an entire community's sense of stability, security and safety, and are perpetuated as part of a chronic cycle. There is a strong body of research to suggest that crime ("*harm done to others*") destabilizes the economic and social structure of communities. When people harm others, it typically creates fear and a general sense of alienation from participation in life. The amount of harm one experiences coincides with the amount of fear they will experience. This fear disrupts individual lives, keeping a person from ever experiencing life to the fullest. In some cases, the fear may severely impede an individual's ability to function. There is also strong evidence linking chronic childhood abuse (a crime, "*harm done to others*", and illegal) with severe forms of psychosis.

THE ROLE OF INTEGRITY

If you have harmed another human being in any of the ways mentioned, and you are willing to make an amends, you are heading the voice of your conscience and integrity. In some instances, you will be able to repair the harm, and in some, you will not be able to do anything about what you did, except to never put yourself in that situation again. Integrity and willingness are your step-stools to take Step Eight.

If you have harmed someone in a way that cannot be fixed, I remind you that the task at hand is only to identify *to whom* the harm was done, and *what* was done to harm them. Even if you cannot repair the harm done, direct, face-to-face verbal amends in which you acknowledge what you did, how it impacted the other person and the change you will make because of it, has great power. First of all, you need this process in order to grow spiritually, and secondly, for those to whom you make an amends to; it can be a longed-for consolation. What you want to avoid, **at all costs**, is giving an inadequate apology, and not change what you originally did to cause the person(s) harm.

With this approach, making amends is about learning how to feel equal with others, relinquishing all attitudes of superiority, making others feel scared of you, or creating the need to avoid you. You can look people in the eye. You no longer have to avoid those you injured out of guilt or shame, fear of being found out, or punished for some reason. Step Eight will bring you to your rightful place among your fellow humans.

THE PERSONAL BENEFITS OF STEP EIGHT

Step Eight affords you the opportunity to listen to someone else's side of the experience, and if they choose, to forgive you. That is profoundly healing for both of you. It is not healthy to hold on to unhealthy residue from interactions with people. Since you are always interacting with people, there is always ample opportunity to cause and feel resentments. Therefore, you need a tool to manage this aspect of life. It is human nature, to hold on to resentments and unprocessed rage, and then act them out. This "acting out", is called *repetition compulsion*; making the same mistake repeatedly while trying to elicit a certain outcome. You make amends so that you can offer yourself the chance to release what happened in the past.

If you are still unsure which people you need to put on your list, a helpful tip is to put all those people that you would prefer not to run into at a social event. Once you complete your list, you have your chance to move forward. This does not necessarily mean that the people on your list have something to forgive *you* for. **But instead, some of the people on your list are related to reasons that you need**

to forgive yourself. Here you are going to rid yourself of your burden as much as you can.

Step Eight allows you to examine if your burden is about harm you have done to another through your own self-centeredness, or if you simply need to forgive yourself. List those people that you brought out the worst in, or those whom you have thrown off balance. If you find yourself overwhelmed with the things you have done to harm others, please take a moment now to say to yourself that you were just wounded and trying to cope. You are not bad, wrong, stupid, crazy, sick, or useless. You always tried to do your best with the tools and knowledge you had. You were trying to survive. You may have been attempting to flee from someone inflicting terrible pain on you. That was then, and this is the present moment. Put yourself *on the top of the list* if you are seeking your own forgiveness for harming yourself.

In Step Four you acknowledged who harmed *you*. In Step Eight you list those whom *you* harmed. This is the beginning of learning how to live in harmony and fairness with yourself and others. This creates peace of mind, which everyone needs.

PAUSE TO REVIEW AND REFLECT

Do you have peace of mind?

_____

_____

If yes, what are your indicators?

_____

_____

If no, why do you not have peace of mind?

THE BENEFITS OF STEP EIGHT FOR HUMANITY

Step Eight is critical for humanity. Here is why: Each year there are millions of Americans who become victims of crime (*harm done to them*). Some of those people harmed by others are able to keep going in life. However, there are those people who require extensive support and community services, that the perpetrator cannot provide (*harms you cannot repair*).

Consequences of causing harm to another human being may include the survivor experiencing continuing psychological suffering and or dysfunction, significant loss of self-confidence, diminished productivity in work or academic performance, suicide, depression, anxiety, various addictions, or mental illness. There is enough evidence to demonstrate that harming another human being, to varying degrees, can impact the person in powerful ways, and can have outcomes that affect the person's health, financial stability, social dysfunction, poor self-esteem, poor coping skills, or impede their overall well-being.

THE BEST POSSIBLE RELATIONSHIP

I put myself on top of my Eighth Step list, and saw that I legitimately had reasons to amend my behaviors, and seek my own forgiveness. I began with ceasing my connection to all the labels that my abusers projected on to me. This initiated the process of evaluating what falsehoods I was harboring about myself. Such falsehoods unconsciously keep me bound and tied psychologically, and my own forgiveness (release from debts owed) was in order.

The beginning of self-amends starts by identifying how your lack of accepting personal responsibility caused harm to your health, financial stability, relationships with others, self-confidence, self-image, relationship with your Higher Power, family, and friends. Following this, is putting an end to any kind of destructive or irresponsible behavior. For example, labeling yourself or others has significant impact, depending on the label given. If you have given yourself or anyone else labels examine them now, and consider being label-free.

Labels I have given myself, or anyone else.	Can I consider being label-free, including not distributing them on to others?

Step Eight has been the beginning of what is described in the *Twelve Steps and Twelve Traditions* of AA as the start of *"the best possible relations with every human being we know."* This must start with you, and letting go of labels and other people's limiting ideas about yourself and others.

The way to achieve *"the best possible relations"* always involves treating people with application of The Golden Rule: *treat people in the manner in which you want to be treated.* Unless the person or situation is abusive, this will involve relating to people with honesty and respect. Take a moment now to list all the people you would like to treat with more respect and honesty. This may also be an opportunity for you to list those people that are toxic in your life, and that you wish to no longer engage with.

Names of toxic people in my life, in light of what I now know and feel.	Can I consider being free from them, either by how I treat them, or by disconnecting from them entirely?

After you have completed this as thoroughly as you can, answer the following questions:

1) In which relationship do you suspect you are not being true to yourself?

_____

_____

2) Are you abusive in any way to anyone including yourself? How?

_____

_____

3) Do you have a tendency to revolve your life around a certain person or relationship?

_____

_____

4) Do you have a tendency to be inappropriately or excessively involved in someone else's life?

_____

_____

5) Do you use seemingly positive traits as a subtle way to control or manipulate people or situations?

_____

_____

6) Are you uncomfortable with the thought of making amends to a particular person in your life? Why?

_____

_____

7) With which people do you feel you cannot be real and relaxed with?

8) a) Are you emotionally distant from your loved ones, leaving them no choice but to assume how you feel, what you need and what you want?

b) When this happens, do you recognize that perhaps your loved one attempts to please you, engage you, or draw you out, but are met by your disapproval or your indifference?

c) Can you see the connection between your emotional distance, and your loved ones feeling hurt, rejected, and blaming themselves for having pushed you away?

_____

_____

9) How do you feel having completed these exercises?

_____

_____

PRAY FOR THE WILLINGNESS TO BE WILLING

There are some trauma survivors who do not believe they are capable of changing. Some are blocked by fear that they cannot change (no matter how sincere is their desire for change). Some have never kept their promises to change, and some really want to stop doing the same thing over and over again, but do not have the faith required to move forward with Step Eight. For such people, there is a well-quoted saying in Twelve Step meetings: *"pray for the willingness to be willing"*. This applies to having faith that the God of your personal understanding will give you the ability and strength to change.

If you have identified certain amends that you cannot see yourself ever making, such as: lack of compassion for the person, there was mutual harm done in the relationship, your level of resentment at the person, or lack of willingness to forgive, keep those on your list. Since you do not have to make your amends all in one day or within a prescribed time limit, you can refer back to your list as often as you need to, and pray for the willingness to become willing...

THE ROLE OF SPIRITUAL QUALITIES IN STEP EIGHT

HONESTY

I recently stated that being able to put this list together signifies integrity and willingness. Step Eight also calls upon you to focus on several key spiritual qualities: compassion, honesty, willingness, and courage. It bears mentioning here that the Twelve Steps are not a religion and not affiliated with any religion or specific doctrine. You *do not* need to accept a specific belief system, doctrine, or religion. However, you *do need* to be honest, courageous, willing, and compassionate.

Spiritual principles are defined as attributes of the spirit that are visible in a person's character. These attributes of the spirit have enormous value, influencing your process of recovery and your life. As I see it, if you follow a specific religion, doctrine, or belief system, remember that ANY doctrine and religious belief are secondary to the spiritual principles themselves. I am mentioning this here because there are survivors who have been victims of religious abuse, and where there is mention of anything spiritual, such as spiritual principles, such people may be triggered to believe that this process involves dogma or religion. Unfortunately, for some survivors of religious trauma, the preoccupation with defending themselves from further such abuses can stunt their development of all things *spiritual*, instead of promoting these essential qualities in their healing journey.

You need to be honest to even begin this process; to admit that in some way your life is unmanageable, without meaning, without direction, and negatively affected by any traumatic experiences. You then acknowledged the solution to your difficulties (Steps Two and Three). This was followed with the Fourth Step; a searching and fearless moral inventory, itemizing your strengths and weaknesses. Certainly all these exercises call for absolute honesty; not an easy task when you are called to take your honesty to such a deep level. There will always be psychological defense mechanisms that can get in the way of your absolute honesty. Denial, for example, is a very common, primitive, and powerful defense mechanism. If you can go behind the back of your ego, and choose absolute honesty, you will more easily distinguish your role in events from other people's role in what happened. This is the fabric of Step Eight; applying an absolute honesty principle so that your ego will not keep you stuck with resentments, a victim-blaming mentality, rationalization preventing you from taking personal responsibility, and any other justification stopping you from placing the appropriate individuals on your Eight Step Amends list.

COURAGE

When you put yourself *in the care of your* Higher Power you are practicing courage. It is oh so tempting to write a list that includes only those people whom you think will respond favorably to you. The trust that you developed in Steps Two and Three will carry you through this phase that requires you to believe that your Higher Power will be there for you every step of the way. This core recovery work requires courage to change the things you can. It takes courage to acknowledge and face the harms you have done. You must feel the fear, do it anyway, and accept the consequences. All this requires the help of a loving God supporting your process through "people, places, and things".

WRITING EXERCISE: MY RELATIONSHIP WITH COURAGE

Write some examples when courage helped you get through something that you did not think you could get through successfully.

_____

_____

_____

_____

COMPASSION

It is essential that you develop a compassionate spirit (not self-pity, blame, or co-dependence) for yourself and others. The word compassion is often misinterpreted as "feeling sorry" or "feeling bad". However, I define it as the Buddhists teach it: compassion is comprised of two words: *'co'* which is defined as *together* and *'passion'*, which is defined as *strong emotion*. You apply compassion (strong emotion) when you make an amends to someone for the harm *you* caused to *them*, bearing witness to their distress and pain. You allow yourself to feel *their* pain as if it were your own, and endeavor to eradicate or at least to reduce their pain.

There are other expressions of compassion which include the three C's: Concern, Caring, and Comfort. Such expressions of compassion play a significant role in meeting face-to-face with those you have hurt, expressing concern for their welfare. Compassion will also nurture your spiritual development, so you can blossom naturally into the person you were meant to be prior to the traumatic events.

You also demonstrate compassion when you think before you speak, when you consider other people's feelings, and when you refrain from responding with rage or resentment at other people's shortcomings.

When others react to you in a way that feels infuriating or annoying, you know that they are misreading the situation, and therefore over-reacting or under-reacting to what is going on. Every person has dreams, faults, passions, longings, fears, needs, desires, and gifts. On a basic level, you are all connected with the Golden Thread of Life, and that alone is reason to feel compassion when you least want to extend it. It is necessary to repeat again that your safety and sanity comes first. **_Please do not put yourself in situations that are harmful, abusive, or toxic, mistaking this for being compassionate._** With every step in this book, it is crucial that you review and discuss your plans with a safe and experienced person, who understands the impact of trauma, and will always advise you to put your safety first. When you work in isolation, you are prone to incorrectly evaluating situations. You must seek the insight, encouragement, feedback, and vision of a trusted advisor.

WRITING EXERCISE: MY RELATIONSHIP WITH COMPASSION

Write some examples when having compassion influenced a difficult situation in a positive, meaningful way.

_____

_____

Trauma and Transformation: A 12-Step Guide.

TWO SURVIVORS SHARE THEIR EXPERIENCE, STRENGTH AND HOPE

Olivia was able to articulate how she harms her two children when her abuse memories are triggered. Her tendency to over-react when her children sneak up on her to hug or play with her, have caused them pain because she would scream and berate them. I explained to her that triggers can be seen as hungry ghosts from the past, and to reframe her children's playfulness as just that: playfulness. Because Olivia reacted beyond what is appropriate for a mother being snuck upon by her two children, this core trigger required introspective examination and support. It reminded her dramatically of how she often felt during her abusive childhood. Having developed this insight Olivia was eager to learn more appropriate responses to her children. She put their names second and third on her list.

Angela's story was similar to many survivors: she was well trained to hide her rage and hurt, keeping the focus on her eagerness to please others. She would go to any length to hold on to a relationship, and was resistant to discussing anything that bothered her. It was easy for her to put on a false smile and pretend she was "fine", no matter what was going on. Angela caused harm to her husband Daniel, when suddenly, after fifteen years of marriage, she asked for a divorce. Daniel was absolutely devastated, and shocked at how unexpected this all was. He was completely blindsided. Angela's emotional dishonesty involved an elaborate and skillful scheme to control, hide, and display only what *she* felt would serve her marriage and home life. Angela had a rude and painful awakening when she took Step Eight. Although she survived a terrible series of traumatic experiences in childhood, she held herself entirely accountable for the harm and damage she caused: *"I know that only hurt people hurt others, but that is still no excuse for me. I want to set this right."* She is still working on making amends, and on forgiving herself.

THE ROLE OF YOUR MOTIVES IN MAKING AMENDS

If you find yourself with the urge to apologize, please take a moment to consider that this urge may be more about your shame than legitimate guilt. There is a simple and effective "acid-test" you can employ *before* making amends to someone: examine your motivation. Before you reach out to make an amends, answer the following four critical questions. Review your answers with wise, loving, competent and compassionate counsel; someone who will not minimize nor invalidate your traumatic history.

1) Are you making amends because you did something wrong?

_____

_____

2) Is your motive to control the other person?

_____

_____

3) Do you expect to receive some payoff?

_____

_____

4) Making amends is about you changing your behavior, which is not easy. **It is not about simply saying "I'm sorry" and moving on.** Are you prepared to change your behavior before adding the person's name to your list?

_____

_____

Learning and practicing new, healthier ways of relating to people can feel frightening. It requires acknowledgment and action that is not centered on addictive impulses. It also means releasing character defects such as shame, blame, or self-centeredness. When you are willing to take appropriate responsibility for your behavior, you will develop the ability to form and maintain solid and healthy relationships. This is one of the fundamental rewards of applying yourself diligently to this entire process; fear, doubt, anxiety, and all the rest of the uncomfortable emotions that tag along.

WRITING EXERCISE

Before you proceed with the Step Eight writing exercise, remember that this step is about identifying the damage *you yourself* are responsible for. It is not fulfilled if you intend in any way to punish someone. Nor should it be motivated by anger, selfishness, or control. Remember: if you caused any damage by your words or deeds, directly or indirectly, that is what gets put on your Eighth Step list.

Complete four separate amends lists: title each one, in order, as follows: 1) "**Right Now**", 2) "**Later**", 3) "**Maybe**", and 4) "**Never!**" On your first list, place the names of the people that you love, and have caused hard to, and are ready right now to balance it out. On your second list ("Later"), place the names of those people that you do not feel motivated to make an amends to them. On your third list ("Maybe"), put the names of those people that you are not sure about. On your fourth list ("Never!") put down the names of those people that you will never make amends to.

> *TIP:*
>
> If you are having a hard time knowing who belongs on your amends list, make a list of your character defects, and ask whom you have hurt by each one of them.

Trauma and Transformation: A 12-Step Guide.

EIGHTH STEP AMENDS LIST – SAMPLE CHART

RIGHT NOW	LATER	MAYBE	NEVER!

TWELVE QUESTIONS FOR CONSIDERATION AND REVIEW

1. Do I owe an amends to someone who can be a potential threat to my safety, or who fills me with apprehension? Describe. (If it feels unsafe to make amends to a particular person, seek wise counsel before taking any action).

_____

_____

_____

_____

2. Do I have resentments that stand in my way of making amends to someone on my list?

_____

_____

_____

_____

3. Is there a situation in which we mutually harmed each other? **Yes/No**. Am I am not willing to make my amends to them because they should make amends to me first? **Yes/No** If no, can I add their names to my list anyway, and pray for the willingness to do my part? **Yes/No**

_____
_____
_____
_____

4. Have I harmed someone, who does not know that I harmed them, but will find out when I approach them? **Yes/No**

_____
_____
_____
_____

5. Who did I harm, and how specifically have I harmed this person? (Financial, physical, sexual, emotional, psychological, or spiritual?)

_____

_____

_____

_____

6. What is the purpose and value of taking responsibility for *the exact nature of my wrongs*?

_____

_____

_____

_____

7. When is my apology, on its own, enough to restore the damage that I caused?

_____

_____

_____

_____

8. What would my life look like if I made amends appropriately?

_____

_____

_____

_____

9. How will Courage and Absolute Truthfulness help me with this step?

_____

_____

_____

_____

10. Is my list complete? If not, am I willing to add them now? (Are you too afraid or resentful to add certain people?)

_____

_____

_____

_____

11. What affect does my traumatic history have on my willingness to practice the spiritual principles linked to Step Eight?

_____

_____

_____

_____

12. Do I feel any more compassion, empathy and connection with people at this point in my journey?

Trauma and Transformation: A 12-Step Guide.

_____

_____

_____

_____

"They tell me: If you see a slave sleeping, do not wake him lest he be dreaming of freedom. I tell them: If you see a slave sleeping, wake him and explain to him freedom." [8]

---

[8] Gibran, Kahlil. *The Treasured Writings of Kahlil Gibran*, (New York: Castle Books, 2010), Pg. 786.

STEP NINE

Made direct amends to such people wherever possible, except when to do so would injure them or others.

Step Nine is no different than the other steps, and it reminds you once again, that you cannot overcome personal difficulty alone. You have prayer as your constant companion to get you through. You pray for the willingness to be willing, whenever you find yourself not willing to take the next right action. If you have people on your list where there has been, or still is, mutual harm being done, you may have difficulty with this step. There may be people on your list for whom you do not feel it necessary to make amends. You may simply not want to. It is advisable, again after consulting with a trusted advisor, that you start making amends to those folks on your *"Right Now"* list. After you have completed this, you will be ready to continue on to the second list. After you have made amends to those people on your second list, you can consider those people on your third list. And finally, you will re-visit making amends to those people on your last list, the "*Never!*" column. The process of *becoming* willing, allows you to prepare yourself for this work through prayer, and through the use of any tools that support your efforts to overcome personal roadblocks.

Let us take a closer look at Step Nine. The first thing is that you could never take this next step if you did not sufficiently prepare yourself spiritually up to this point. This spiritual preparation involves admitting your limitations, developing a relationship with a Higher Power, writing and turning over the Fourth Step Inventory, and developing humility. The humility you develop by taking the Sixth and Seventh Steps helps you to have clarity in your personal responsibilities. It is good and strength-based to be responsible, and no one, regardless of personal trauma history, should be dismissed from this. Without this approach, you may do more harm in the Eighth and Ninth Steps, (perhaps out of anger or self-righteousness).

The first thing you can see is that it is a three-part step that is clear with the instructions of which kind of amends to make. The first part is the instruction on **how** to make them: *"made direct amends"*. This refers to amends that are made face to face, and in a direct manner, with the person. Here you will avoid any passive-aggressive means, such as hinting, indirect statements, any subtle manipulation to try and get the person to see their part of the harm, to avoid some part of it, or anything that is other than direct, face-to-face, candid and real. The second instruction is **when** to make them: *"wherever possible"*. This is very straightforward, and does not afford any room for vagueness or loop-holes. The third instruction is when **not** to make them: *"except when to do so would injure them or others"*.

What if you need to make an amends to someone that you hate? Making a direct amends can seem impossible at its worst, and overwhelming at its best. Here is where you consult with your Higher Power, and a trusted advisor, to guide you in approaching such a person. Following wise counsel, and obtaining helpful information, can prevent you from causing any harm. It is important to be mindful that you may have a lot of zeal in pursuing this step, and are eager to expose the skeletons in the closet so you can be free of them. However, without careful thought, planning, and prayer, you can end up harming instead of helping.

Some survivors pursue this step impulsively, because they are seeking to escape their underlying shame and guilt over the harm that they caused. Step Nine becomes about *their* self-centered desire to escape their shame and guilt, as opposed to real understanding of the harm *they caused* to *someone else*. To avoid this common pitfall, seriously considering of *what was the harm*, will serve as a guide to determine if you owe an amends. It may be that you actually need to otherwise process your own guilt or shame around your actions.

Therefore, you remind yourself that the simple goal of Step Nine is to brush away debris from *your* side of the street, not *their* side of the street. The purpose of making amends is **not** to get the person to like you. **This means that you never tell the person you are making an amends to, how they should feel or respond. You do not find fault with them, or criticize them in any way. You simply stick to your part, and once you do so, it is over with.** There may be times when you make amends, which will result in healing a relationship, but no amends should depend on that, because the other person's reactions are their right, and cannot be predicted. To minimize the chances of you feeling humiliation, pain, or rejection, I suggest that you remove any expectations about how your amends will be responded to by the recipient.

The Ninth Step is like a powerful electric saw. If you make amends properly, Step Nine can be used to repair relationships (beginning with yourself), and to build relationships (if this is the natural outcome of that exchange). However, if you lose control, you can injure yourself and damage others. It is well worthwhile to learn how to use Step Nine as cautiously and thoroughly as you would before using an electric saw. This applies no matter how much experience you have using power tools. There is an expression for using power tools that I find to be applicable: *"Measure twice, cut once!"*

The benefit of *direct amends* is that if you make amends directly, eye-to-eye, you are sure of how the person received your amends. With indirect amends, you may remain preoccupied with what you will say or do the next time you see the person. You may continue to doubt if you really did your utmost to make amends. This can happen as a result of making amends over the phone or by electronic means. However, if you make amends in person, you are through with it and you will never have to worry about it again. There is no doubt that making *direct amends* is the best way to go about it! Even if the person has a strong reaction to you, this is the worst that you will experience, and now you do not have to worry, obsess, or create scenarios about what would happen, could happen, or should happen.

A WORD OF CAUTION

If the person becomes unsafe to you, please leave and get help if necessary. If the person has their own strong reaction, hear them out. Give them a chance to air their pain, or unresolved feelings regarding the hurt you caused them. If you are concerned with the person's feelings, hard as it might be for you, accept their right to complain. Listen, care, and feel your own pain at what you contributed to. At that point, you will deeply apologize for what you did, with a specific action plan to change your behavior so you do not repeat the same mistake. You may need some time and more specific guidance, but you should at least try. This is healing for the both of you.

There are also the amends of paying back what you owe in equal amount, otherwise referred to as equal restitution amends. If you stole anything, and never paid it back, if you wrote bad checks, broke something that belonged to someone, ran up bills, or otherwise engaged in fraudulent, dishonest, or damaging behavior, it is useless to just verbally admit to it and say "I am sorry". The person you have just confessed to will undoubtedly want back what you stole/destroyed/damaged. It is natural to feel apprehension if you are going to face somebody that you owe something to. If you are experiencing overwhelming fear, you may want to break down the amends into manageable parts. For example, if you owe someone a sum of money that you can ill afford to pay, you can offer to pay a certain sum of money every week. Choose a dollar amount that you can afford, and try not to be ashamed of that amount, because eventually the money you owe will get paid. Taking this one action-step will help to mitigate, or even eliminate your fear, guilt and remorse, as you take a constructive approach to each amends owed.

AMENDS FOR THE SEXUAL ABUSE OF A MINOR(S)

There are those trauma survivors who have committed the felony crime of sexually abusing a minor and wish to make amends. They have diligently worked Steps One through Eight sought the counsel of trusted advisors, have admitted to perpetrating this crime, and are receiving the right treatment. Making amends face-to-face is the best way to make amends *wherever possible*. However, direct amends in some cases, may be the worst way, and it is not the only way to make amends. The discussion that follows on this highly painful subject are only *suggestions*, and as with this entire book, is not ever meant to take the place of a wise, competent, and safe person who will review your specific situation, and work with you to make a decision on what is the best process for all concerned.

Pedophilia is a very serious disorder, requiring the proper treatment, and possible medication. If you are seeking to make amends because you sexually abused a minor (this precludes children who explore each other without the intent to harm), the first step is to seek appropriate guidance, **before taking any action**. There is no obvious or simple solution, and for some harms done, the ONLY amend is to never repeat it, get the right help so you can enforce your commitment, and pray for your victim's healing and success in life.

ADMISSION: SOME CONSIDERATIONS

Making amends for sexually abusing a minor will not start your victim's healing process, and s/he may absolutely refuse to agree to it. The person has to be ready and willing, and strong enough in their own journey, to receive your amends if they choose to. **If your victim is still a minor, this should not be done without the consent of the victim, the consent of the minor's guardian, and without the presence of well-trained, licensed, compassionate mental health professional(s) who will place the needs of the victim above all else. In any amends process involving a victim, the needs of your victim must be the main concern, and neither you, nor anyone else involved,**

should ever force or coax the victim to partake in your plan to make amends. If there is any fear from the victim towards you, or an imbalance of power on any level, the victim may easily be dominated, which can further traumatize this person.

If you want to make amends to your victim, just to apologize quickly so you can move on, but do not believe you did anything wrong, speak to a well-trained professional with experience in these matters **before you take any further action.** Do not do anything that will re-traumatize, or further traumatize your victim. To do further damage to the person is a highly selfish act on your part; **not at all in the spirit of the Ninth Step Amends.** Victims, especially if they are minors, can be weak or frightened and may give in to the pressure to "forgive and forget". This usually results in their not adequately processing their pain and anger, which can further damage them. Remember, that you as the perpetrator of these sexual harms are **not** on equal footing with non-sexual offenders nor with your victims. It is also not a requirement for you to face your victim in person, if this will cause harm to him/her. Some alternate options include:

1) Writing (mailed or simply kept for your own records) an empathy letter for your victim, where you ONLY admit to what you did, and affirm the damage you caused, and their pain and suffering.

2) Through an appropriate sex-offender treatment program, you seek and maintain the help you need to uphold your genuine commitment to amend your behavior.

The goal of making amends, if you sexually abused a minor, is for the recovery of the victim. This is different than making amends for harms that are in a different category. The reason for this is that crimes of a sexual nature cause specific and very deep suffering. The injuries cannot be mended by writing a check or a brief apology. Since your victim has already suffered terribly, you want to take every precaution not to create any more pain and suffering. For this reason, face-to-face amends may not be advisable or possible. You, as the perpetrator of such a heinous act, have to acknowledge and admit your abusive and illegal act, **and you must hold yourself accountable**. The amends must begin by never perpetrating such offensive criminal behavior. Other minors should be protected from you and you should receive proper clinical treatment immediately. This must be your first order of business if you are sincere about making amends.

If you have followed all of these suggestions thus far, exactly as I have described, and your victim has readily agreed to meet with you, under the supervision of a properly trained professional, there can be some significant advantages. This is an opportunity for your victim to confront you with how *your* acts affected ***them***. They can express to you some of the pain and rage that they had to suffer silently, and they can assert that they will no longer protect your secret. With such a confrontation with you, and with the freedom to say to you any variation of the following: *"You had no right to do what you did; I know exactly what you did to me"* this person is no longer being controlled by what you did, is no longer silenced, and finally can cry out their pain.

If you will be meeting with your victim face-to-face to make amends, please carefully observe the following three critical guidelines (***which can be applied to making amends of any kind and not just sexual***):

1) The victim must decide that they are **completely ready,** and are not participating out of any sense of obligation, guilt or fear. **You need to be *absolutely sure* about this before proceeding.** Ask them if they

are in any these states, which is highly likely if there is any power imbalance between the both of you. **YOU** did the damage, so do not force yourself on the victim, **EVEN IF** your intentions are noble.

2) Making amends to your victim should be about honoring their feelings, pain and suffering. If you feel the need to protect yourself and you do not want the possibility of being challenged during the conversation, you are not in a position of strength to face your accuser. Your apology needs to be heartfelt, and if you doubt that what you did was wrong, further soul-searching on your part may be in order first. If you do not feel genuine remorse or empathy, you are obligated to keep your distance. Pray for their healing, but from a distance. **Do not expect your victim to pardon you of YOUR guilt -that is NEVER their job.** The person is at liberty to leave at any time,

and /or not to have anything further to do with you. Remember that no person who sexually abuses a minor is doing the best they can **UNDER ANY CIRCUMSTANCES!** If you have committed such a grave criminal and moral offense, you have violated a human being weaker and smaller than you. You have violated a sacred trust, robbed them of their bodies, and violated their mind and soul. **Do not EVER make your victim responsible for YOUR feelings.** That is manipulation, laying guilt and blame, it is dishonest, selfish, and has no place in the amends process. If you believe that your victim is responsible for your feelings, do not bother trying to make amends. You will be causing harm instead of an amends. **If you are the parent or sibling who committed incest, you are not excused just because you have a biological connection to your victim.**

3) Do not offer a quick, easy, fast apology; which is only about ending your own uncomfortable feelings. Your victim has the right to know what happened, and has the right to express their anger to the fullest extent. Respect this right, and avoid minimizing their anger in any way. That would be highly insulting and cruel.

4) If you seek your victim's forgiveness, you should earn it. You earn forgiveness by acknowledging what you did WITHOUT minimization, excuses, stories, or rationalization. You provide the space for your victim to fully and openly detail *their experience* of the abuse. Do not rush or pressure them into finishing. Accept his/her right to complain bitterly and extensively. After you have listened, express care and empathy for the pain you caused your victim. You can now apologize for your crimes. DO NOT APOLOGIZE, at this point, if you feel any

sense of pleasure from bearing witness to their suffering, or feel any arrogance or entitlement from your victim.

CONSEQUENCES OF MAKING AMENDS

There are certain actions when admitted to the victim, may result in you going to jail, termination of employment, a break-up of a family or significant relationship, or other critical outcomes. Since each situation needs to be carefully evaluated (seek legal advice if necessary), it is best if you do not rush into taking any action. There is an oft-quoted saying in twelve step circles: *"When in doubt – leave it out!"* Explore your options, but as with any harm committed, **you need to accept the consequences of the harms <u>you did</u>**. The Ninth Step states clearly "*...except when to do so would injure them or others*", and this would clearly apply to anyone who would be affected by your admission and its' attending consequences.

If you stole from a company, or maliciously tried to ruin a business, an example of amends in this case would be to refer customers to the business, anonymously pay back stolen money, do volunteer or charity work for the benefit of this organization, or find other honest, creative ways that provide equal restitution.

If the person to whom you owe amends has passed away, you can make amends by compensating their children, making financial donations in the deceased's name, or any other action that feels genuine. Since you are influenced by your spiritual beliefs, culture, the nature of the harm, or the level of willingness, you will respond according to each situation. If you cannot locate the person, you may want to extend your best effort to locate this person, and in the interim, *take great care* not to repeat the harmful behavior to others. If you caused harm while under the influence of a substance, your primary amend is to get abstinent from that substance, and do everything you can to stay abstinent. Otherwise, you will repeat the same problematic behaviors. Remain open and willing to correct this wrong, and remember that your Higher Power is always present and available to assist you.

As you proceed through your list, **pay attention to which person or harm done is causing you the most intense fear, guilt, or remorse**. If this feels too overpowering, remind yourself that the painful feelings are temporary. If you let them block you, you will remain stuck repeating the same behaviors. You will continue to be burdened with buried remorse. Usually the areas of your life that causes you the most overwhelming emotions are the most significant ones. If you avoid them, you remain stuck and never move forward in healing. Unprocessed emotions such as deep shame, guilt, fear, remorse, and disappointment create an inner trap that keep you stuck. It is crucial to your recovery to examine such feelings as they arise in you.

Examine their origins, the role they play in your life, and the message they have for you.

You can think of Step Nine as the step that assists you in liberating the toxins buried inside yourself. If you were cleaning out your trash, you would not be satisfied with just writing a list of all your garbage, rotting meat, decaying food, etc. You would absolutely have to take the garbage away from you, so it can properly be disposed of. Unprocessed fear, guilt, shame, and remorse can sit inside of you, decaying and spreading inner poison. Such toxic feelings can cause you to repeat the very things you are trying to keep "hidden"! So in effect, whatever you are trying to keep hidden, actually never stays hidden, but comes out "sideways" via symptoms, resentments, physical ailments, disappointing relationships, etc. What a paradox of the human psyche!

Perhaps you are a prideful person, and believe that if you make amends, you will be depleted in some way or lose out. If you are rejected, perhaps you fear that faith in the process will be devastated. This is understandable. But the fact is that by removing your blockages, **you will prosper.** You will prosper because you are eliminating your debts, and will feel much more comfortable with yourself. This may be a good time to return to Step Three, and remember that your Higher Power is with you all the time. If you are sincere and can step aside so your Higher Power can help you, you will find yourself with the tools to make necessary repairs in your life - courtesy of the Divine Magistrate.

YOUR REACTION WHEN MAKING AMENDS

When you are in front of the person, remember to remain humble and concrete. You may feel eager for them to accept you, and to forgive your wrongdoing. If the person chooses to reject your efforts to make amends, you may feel utterly crushed and humiliated. You may feel compelled, or actually, go back repeatedly to beg their forgiveness. Although this is perfectly human, please remember that if someone does not accept your efforts, there is nothing you can do about it. Try to let it go. *You made an honest and very courageous effort that most people probably would never try.* This is a huge step in your own spiritual growth, and in transforming your past actions.

If you are one of those people who put themselves in situations where they wind up being rejected repeatedly; remember that every time you go back to try for a particular reaction from someone, you cause yourself to pay the price of feeling bad over and over again. It is fair to assume that by the time you face the person, you already paid a huge price in physical, spiritual, or emotional turmoil. You can refuse this cycle of paying and paying forever. Some people, due to their own character flaws, will allow you to pay forever. However, if you are aligned with your Higher Power, with yourself, and with others in your life, on a healthy path, you will find healing and sanity in the Three Dimensions of Life (God, Myself, and Others). I say this to emphasize that even if strong negative feelings are triggered by someone rejecting you, you are still on the right track. Try not to let someone's reaction, triggers, issues, character defects or moods interrupt this critical phase of development.

As a result of taking such powerful actions thus far, you may experience a spiritual awakening. Such an awakening is the result of freeing your mind of the unhealthy guilt, shame, and remorse as a result of causing harm to others. You will no longer experience the same kind of confusion that accompanies such a burden of guilt. You will also come to appreciate that the Twelve Steps are designed for you to take, one at a time, just like you take the stairs to get to a higher level.

This process will trigger a fear of letting go and a fear of the unknown. There can be such vulnerability, that you may sometimes wonder, why even bother? You "bother" because this process makes you a better person. You will lose the compulsion to engage in wrongful behavior. At this point, your awareness of the consequences of harmful behavior to yourself and others may include an awareness of human misery and its attending pain. You will begin to care more and feel less angry. You will become forgiving, less selfish, more loving and compassionate for yourself and others. The benefits and blessings of this work are extraordinary.

PUTTING YOURSELF AND GOD ON THE LIST

You start to amend your relationship with yourself by not continuing unhealthy patterns, relationships, behavior, or toxic thinking. You further your growth by acting in accordance with each step you have taken thus far. These actions will go a long way toward mending the hurt you have done to your soul. There are other healing actions you may need or want to do. This is the time to address any healing that your mind and body needs.

Making amends for neglect of your mind may include learning something new, pursuing education, or furthering your knowledge in some area. You will seek activities that feel constructive and meaningful to you. Making amends to your body includes a healthy diet accompanied by exercise, seeking necessary medical care, yoga, nature walks, or cultivating anything that feels right and healing for your body. Daily prayer and meditation is one way to make amends to God. You honor your Higher Power with anything you do to honor your humanness, care for your mind, body, and soul, as well as for all living things. Making a daily effort to be close to your Creator is amends for a possible lifetime of distancing.

REVIEW AND MOVING AHEAD

The roots of many destructive, unhealthy, or otherwise toxic behavioral patterns, can be traced to prior traumatic experiences. Although this is not always the case, it often is. People are affected by trauma in personal ways. How one is affected depends on the age of when you experienced it, the nature of the experience, and the frequency of occurrence.

CONNECT THE DOTS

Trauma and Transformation: A 12-Step Guide.

Read and answer each question below, connecting the dots from your traumatic experiences, to the amends you are seeking to make.

1) An example of "hidden trauma" is neglect resulting in feeling undeserving of care. Is this true for you?

_____

_____

_____

_____

2) What may have been destroyed in you through the trauma?

_____

_____

_____

_____

3) What harms have you caused by omission (not doing something you should have done?

_____

_____

_____

_____

4) What qualities and adaptations have you developed from having gone through them?

_____

_____

_____

_____

Unhealthy human behavior usually comes from a place of damage; you are likely to pass on what you know, and what was done to you. This is the dark and tragic face of trauma. I firmly believe that if you follow, and truthfully apply this spiritual program of action, you will see that the first nine steps will bring you to an end of your search for your Lost Self. In performing a "deep cleansing" you find what you are looking for. The first nine steps will guide you to do what you require for healing: they bring you back to your True Self, which is *"a spiritual being having a human experience"*. The best part of following a spiritual program of action is that it will never turn against you.

RESPONSIBILITY AND RESTITUTION

As we have been discussing, the word "amend" means to alter. You cannot alter your behavior, unless you first take ownership of it. When you respond appropriately to a wrong you have committed, (by omission or commission), take responsibility AND amend your behavior, you have made a complete amends. ***It does not depend on the other person's reaction, and is not a pass/fail or graded exam.*** You are not responsible for other people's thoughts, feelings or actions, however difficult this may be to internalize.

David told me his experience with taking Step Nine and using it to repair major credit card theft. David stole $15,000 in a credit card scheme when he was a late adolescent. He used to believe that because his father berated and shamed him constantly, that this behavior was an escape, and in some way, excusable. However, by the time he reached his Ninth Step, he felt very differently. He struggled with how to make amends in this case, since he did not have the contact information of those he stole from, and was missing other pertinent information. In order to repair the damage he did, he not only ceased any kind of dishonest behavior, but he was able to set up a payment plan to a charity for needy children, which over a period of time would equal the sum of what he stole. He chose to remain as an anonymous donor, and was able to live free from the burden of guilt and shame.

Tammy, on the other hand, has never stolen a penny from anyone, but when she reviewed her amends list, she was distressed to acknowledge how many people she has alienated in her life through her critical, judgmental, and hostile ways of behaving. She was able to meet face-to-face with some of them, but others refused to speak with her. For some she had no way to make contact. She describes her experience with those she met face-to-face as *"the most terrifying, nerve-wracking thing I ever did; also the most freeing. So glad I did it. I wish I did this much earlier in my life."* For those people whom she could not reach, she resolved to make a living amends by becoming a more sensitive and aware person. She began practicing treating people with consideration, gentleness, and patience. She admitted to me that she struggled for some time with those people who refused to see her, but that she took the opportunity to accept it as a consequence of her own behavior. Today, she holds no grudges, and rarely has a negative word to say about anyone.

Ruth, the mother of twin girls, was surprised to discover that after treating them with more patience and less yelling, they fought less with each other, and were more cooperative at home and in school. While she did not sit down face-to-face with her children to describe her behavior and to apologize, she did keep her promise to be a more loving mother. She describes feeling *"much saner and grounded when I don't yell at or criticize these little innocent angels. It helps me, it helps them, and it gives my partner more peace of mind. We are a more functional family since I made my amends. What a blessing!"*

If you need to make amends to young children, remember that although the face-to-face is important, they may not fully understand what you are saying. Actions always speak louder than words. This is why the power of making amends lies in backing up your words with appropriate actions. This is how you take responsibility for your part in the relationship.

If the harm you have caused is because you said cruel, untrue, or abusive things about another person, and the person(s) would be injured if you revealed this, it is advisable to amend your behavior rather than admit to it. In the spirit of avoiding injury to self and others, resolve to be mindful of everything you say, and how you say it. **Remember if your behavior does not follow your words, you have made a counterfeit claim of remorse. You are both better off without it.**

Survivors have a tendency to assume that their negative feelings toward someone are a reason to make amends. Remember that feelings alone do not cause harm. If you worry a lot about pleasing other people, you may feel that you need to add people to your Eighth Step that do not belong there. The Ninth Step is a good time and place to review such people. If you experienced very strong negative emotions for someone, instead of making amends to them, (which can also be an escape to facing what you are hiding from), you may want to explore if your feelings are a normal response to what occurred between the both of you. If you discover that you have a tendency to avoid anger and sorrow, or turn it into chronic guilt, do not put those people on your amends list. Take the time to work through your feelings, and remind yourself that you are entitled to your feelings, and they do not cause injury to others.

Some survivors owe amends to themselves for abusing their bodies. Perhaps you harmed your body, as an escape from dealing with unresolved feelings caused by the trauma. You can begin the amends process by taking actions to restoring your body, such as proper nutrition, sufficient rest, and regular exercise (as already mentioned).

When you face what you have been avoiding, and change old behavioral patterns, you will stop living a life of hide-and-go-seek with yourself. You will be available for close and honest relationships, and you will experience relationships based on trust and truth. As the Buddhist saying goes: *"What you run from will chase you, and what you chase, will run from you."* This is the greatest gift of the Ninth Step. There will be no more running, chasing, or hiding. You face those people and your behaviors that you were so afraid to face. The fears transform from being monsters in the closet, to becoming strength and vitality for connection.

The Ninth Step is the end of the road for a life of "repetition compulsion". Human beings continually re-enact the old, destructive, trauma-based behaviors they have learned. It is truly the dawn of a new day. If you long for this new day, for a life of meaningful, honest, grounded, real connections, achieving this step is worth the experience of humility. You will find that it is not demeaning, but uplifting. If you feel ready, let us move on to Step Ten.

> ***"It isn't that to have an honorable relationship with you, I have to understand everything, or tell you everything at once or that I can know, beforehand, everything I need to tell you.***
> ***It means that most of the time I am here, longing for the possibility of telling you. That these possibilities may seem frightening, but not destructive, to me. That I feel strong enough to hear your tentative and groping words. That we both know we are trying, all the time, to extend the possibilities of truth between us.***
> ***The possibility of life between us."*** [9]

---

[9] Rich, Adrienne, *On Lies, Secrets & Silence: Selected Prose* 1966-1978. (New York: Norton, 1979), Pgs. 183-84.

STEP TEN

Continued to take personal inventory and when we were wrong promptly admitted it.

Step Ten is not about maintenance, because there is a rule in our universe that nothing ever stays the same. All living matter is either in a process of growing or in the process of regressing. Up until now, if you followed the first nine steps with an honest heart and the direction of a Higher Power, you will have grown considerably. If you do not keep growing, you will start sliding back into your old behavior patterns and ways of thinking.

As you may now realize, spiritual growth is an experience so precious and valuable. As with the preceding nine steps, the Tenth Step is one more power-tool to help you succeed during the day. Let us take a closer look at how Step Ten is helpful to you right now. If you are someone prone to anger, anxiety (intra-psychic conflicts), resentment, depression, or fear, do not wait until bedtime to process it. Do a Tenth Step inventory <u>right away</u>. Begin by saying a prayer (the Serenity Prayer is a popular choice), in order to move through the moment:

> **GOD GRANT ME THE SERENITY TO ACCEPT THE THINGS I CANNOT CHANGE, COURAGE TO CHANGE THE THINGS I CAN, AND WISDOM TO KNOW THE DIFFERENCE.**[10]

---

[10] *Twelve Steps and Twelve Traditions*, (New York: Alcoholics Anonymous World Services, Inc., 1981. (The "Twelve and Twelve."), Pg. 41.

SAMPLE TENTH STEP INVENTORY

My name: Today's Date:	
State the incident in one sentence.	
What was my underlying motivation, and involvement?	
Which of my strengths did I utilize in this incident?	Examples: Honest, giving, faithful, open-minded, flexible, gentle, patient, present emotionally, sensitive, caring, avoid shaming or hurting at all costs, encouraging, supportive, responsible.
Which of my weaknesses were played out, and how?	Examples: Selfish, resentful, demonstrated a lack of faith, dishonest (by commission or omission), demand to do it my way (control), demand to be right, demand to be a victim ("Poor me"), defiant, in denial ("I don't care, I want it my way"), who did I hurt and how?
How can I correct my mistake?	
If I did_____ the outcomes would have improved.	
"Love and tolerance of others is our code."	**p. 84, Alcoholics Anonymous**

If you are still feeling the emotions intensely, and fear you may do damage because of it, ask your Higher Power to remove the *destructive effect* of this emotion. Praying for the wisdom and courage to process it in a sane (i.e. healthy) way, is always helpful. Remember that feelings are not a moral issue – they are a part of being human and alive. It is what you do with the feelings that determine if a corrective action needs to take place. If after careful consideration of the incident, you have discovered a better way to have responded, attempt to restore the relationship with the person as soon as possible. You will find that if you are reflective and proactive in this manner, you will have more genuine self-regard, and will make the world a better place!

Spiritual growth is about being in touch with your inner world (taking your spiritual temperature), and responding in healthy ways (taking appropriate responsibility for your side of things). When you are in touch with your inner world, you may have an easier time understanding your behavior, and correcting those behaviors that cause harm. If you have a tendency to be self-righteous (insisting that others live according to your values or opinions) and you hurt people because of it, you can now own it, admit it, and not act on it. With this new awareness through the Tenth Step Daily Inventory, you can say *"Yes, I admit that when I get self-righteous, I hurt such and such a person in this particular way"*. You can go back to Step Six and Step Seven so that your character defects do not remain unchecked.

This is your chance to practice *responding*, instead of *reacting*, the next time the urge to be self-righteous comes up. The power in being conscious, in general, is that whatever was controlling you will loosen its grip over you. This includes all the effects of trauma. Part of being conscious is being clear enough to understand your trauma-reactive habits and learning healthier ways of living.

There are some trauma survivors who have a very difficult time admitting that they have certain emotions and character defects. These are the dishonest "nice guys." Such people have the tendency to externalize (show on the outside with their behaviors) a different reaction, such as being nice or friendly, when on the inside, they can be seething. Such emotions, like anger, will come out sideways. People who are Passive-Aggressive or co-dependent are great examples. They pretend they are not angry, when in reality their anger has tremendous power over them. It leaks out like a toxic gas. Such anger, or any such emotions that you have difficulty expressing honestly and without harming someone, will definitely continue to have power and influence over you, until you can *claim* that emotion. For example, if you struggle with anger, you can claim that anger by simply saying out loud, or to another trusted person, "*Yes. I feel anger inside me, and I am willing to hear its message. Maybe this anger I am feeling is about something important, or perhaps it is misleading me."*

In the Serenity Prayer, you pray for *"the wisdom to know the difference"*. If you have discovered the difference for you when you experience anger (I am triggered vs. my anger has a message for me), you can choose to own it, utilize your anger for growth, or simply let go of it. Without the Tenth Step, you are lacking in ongoing healthy self-reflection and humility, which are critical to the total process of growth, regardless of what program of action you follow. When you self-reflect, you keep the doors open within yourself for knowledge of what is real in yourself, other people, and your Higher Power. Step Ten is a potent tool for your life-long journey of fulfilling relationships with yourself, others, and your' Higher Power.

SPIRITUAL PRINCIPLES ARE POWER-TOOLS FOR CHANGE

The three key spiritual principles utilized in this step are integrity, self-discipline, and perseverance. Trauma survivors, like anyone else, are prone to being self-absorbed, fearful, and self-centered. These are basic human character flaws. When traumatized, survivors can stew in these emotions, causing harm to self or others. They have not learned how to process the experience with integrity and self-discipline. If you stew in painful emotions, this choice reinforces itself with familiar feelings of superiority, self-righteousness, or contempt. You may actually love feeling that way because it is comfortable for you, and you can use these feelings to justify avoiding your responsibility in relationships.

A roadblock for most survivors is that you are used to compulsively avoiding what needs to be addressed on the inside. You may get lost in excessive problem-solving to avoid focusing on personal growth and a spiritual solution.

Problem-solving is critical for healthy functioning, but be careful to not avoid your character defects that require you to make a reparation. The Tenth Step may not feel like a good fit for "problem solvers". This is where the honesty you practiced in Step One is fulfilled. To spend some time at the end of every day reviewing your behavior, and necessary amends calls for a depth of honesty, perseverance, and self-discipline. **Having the awareness of when you are right and when you are wrong, is the effective way to change the patterns and habits that cause you difficulty.**

The main object of the Twelve Steps is to find a power greater than yourself that *will* work with you to solve your problems. For example, if your anger is too intense for you to follow the instructions for this step, stop and pray for the anger to be removed. Take a leap of faith when you do not believe these action steps will work for you to remove your character defects. When you start seeing the results in your life, you will start believing in the steps, and you will regularly reach for support to continue this work.

In my personal experience of following a spiritual plan, I discovered that there is one major change from my previous "plans". With my old way, I did a lot of figuring out and analyzing until I thought I found a workable solution to whatever my problem was at that time. When I applied a spiritual program to my personal 'stuck points', my "whys" did not have the same level of significance. There are some areas in yourself and in life where you will never get a satisfactory answer. The object in applying a spiritual program is to be free from your problems, whether or not you "figured them out".

The Tenth Step is not about figuring it all out - it is about having them 'lifted' from you, through prayer, introspection, and being proactive. You may find this concept unacceptable because your mind is wired to figuring things out. However, if you can practice Step Ten on a daily basis, and be content with what is happening in the present moment, you will have created an arch that you will walk under to a place of peace. Regression happens to you when you do not seek a higher way to operate in life, and Step Ten can be what prevents you from regressing. As with each step, you do not do it without adequate support.

Although you are now up to Step Ten, you are going to return to Step One, where you admitted to struggling with your particular dilemmas that are a result of traumatic experiences. For some people, no amount of intellectualizing or analyzing will bring them out of the effects of the trauma, because some effects are simply too intense. You are powerless over anything (person, place, thing, feeling, character trait) that is more powerful than you. Try carrying a Mac Truck on your shoulders. You will not ever be able to lift such a burden with your own bare hands, so you would never in your right mind entertain such an attempt. There are some effects of trauma (fill in the blank for what you are currently struggling with), that you, alone and unaided, cannot fix, resolve, or deal with. For some survivors, it may be the painful awareness of what happened to you, where you were unaided, helpless, powerless, and unable to respond to the situation. **This is NOT a flaw or weakness in you, but rather, a testament to your courageous survival.**

So how does Step Ten help you to manage your personal trauma effects? Knowledge on its own will not help you because you are still powerless over what originally happened. However, when you can start with *that acknowledgment*, you have begun a spiritual program of healing. Some people do not believe in any form of a Higher Power. If that means you, then at least believe in your

Trauma and Transformation: A 12-Step Guide.

situation - **that you did suffer some trauma that affected you in some significant way.** If you really understand that at the time you were powerless over what happened, you can take the next step of getting rid of old ideas. These old ideas are the ones that were formed at that time, and that have been with you ever since. You grow healthier and happier by getting rid of old ideas, and you build character by replacing them with necessary and updated ideas that are true and life-affirming.

Step Ten is your chance to transform an undesirable character trait, because each character defect has a flip side to it, and you can reveal the beauty of it by being willing to pause, reflect, and take necessary action. This step is also where you learn how to reveal your true self, which could still be in hiding. The true self that is within each person, will be revealed by transforming character defects, and following a process of stripping away what you discover to be your false self. This will be achieved, in part, through taking a daily inventory and regularly evaluating what works, what does not, and how you need to be proactive in your growth.

For some of you, there was once a time where you were forbidden to radiate. You may still be abiding by this. This Twelve Step journey is inherently about getting in touch with that part of you, so you can radiate! How delicate and precious this gift is! In addition, you may find that after applying the Twelve Step program, you have found that it is all about the answer to powerlessness. The answer to powerlessness, as you define it, is a Power greater Than Yourself. Each human being has her/his own definition and a personalized answer to this. The obvious solution to being powerless (completely overwhelmed by something, unaided and alone), is to secure for yourself ***a good, reliable source of power***.

When you regularly practice the Tenth Step, you will find that you no longer have a whole list of people you are afraid to run into, a list of events, or emotions that you must avoid. When you are wrong, you promptly admit it, change what is necessary, and move on. This is your daily instruction for living, and is the inventory that goes with Step Two: *"Came to believe that a Power greater than ourselves could restore us to sanity"*. Sanity can be defined as functionally balanced. The Tenth Step inventory is one of the great secrets of staying happy, because happiness is about lifting your personal blockages. Your Fourth and Tenth Step inventories are your personal catalogue of blockages. A lack of happiness is because, in some way, you are disconnected from your channel of serenity. This results in a lack of flow, and it usually manifests itself in the body as well. Step Ten reflects a simple, yet deep understanding of the spiritual view of human behavior.

ROADBLOCKS ALONG YOUR INNER PATH TO TRANSFORMATION

Itemize your inner blockages, as YOU experience it, and not as you have been criticized. Identify areas in the three categories: mental, spiritual, and physical, and consider the following: Blockages are a build-up of unprocessed pain, fear, grief, sadness, loneliness, and anger. Can you name any blockages you are feeling and experiencing? Is it hard for you to sit with this question, and do you just want to magically have this channel opened, and flowing, so you can move onward?

As a preventative measure, I encourage you to take a *'spot-check inventory'* (another term for Tenth Step inventory commonly used in Twelve Step circles), when you first start to notice that you are losing control. If you are one of those survivors who have a hard time facing that you have lost control, try replacing the word *control* with **conscious**

contact. Say to yourself *"I am starting to lose conscious contact with myself, and I am willing to check in with myself to see how I am doing"*. You can also keep the channel open by asking yourself throughout the day: *"In what ways can I grow?"* For some survivors, keeping the channel open during the day means to avoid being mean, critical, or abusive to self and others. Your challenge may be to speak your truth in a sensitive and firm way. (You can also refer to your Fourth Step Inventory to remain clear about your own growth areas).

Remember that your top priority is getting unblocked. This replaces taking revenge, self-destructing, isolating, or choosing to remain ignorant. Use how and what you externalize to guide your plan for attending to your inner world. Your new plan should at least include a spot-check inventory whenever you feel disturbed. Do not waste time worrying about your right to have any of your feelings. They are your feelings. You do not need approval or permission to experience them. They sometimes have messages for you. Other times you are over-reacting or under-reacting. *So remember that the purpose of this spot-check inventory is to name, understand, and dissolve what blocks your flow of serenity.* Dissolving a Serenity-Blockage is done in several ways: (1) Take necessary action, (2) Allow the situation to be as it is, (3) Identify and resolve what you are disturbed by, (4) Pray and seek for support and guidance, and (5) let it go.

As you become comfortable with reviewing your day, and taking corrective action, you may discover a few things that are entirely new to you: 1) You actually enjoy the self-exploration process, 2) You start to feel less numb, compulsive, fearful, out of control, or angry. You are therefore able to release more of the toxic shame and unnecessary guilt that so many survivors carry without even realizing it.

I have found it very helpful to keep a journal along with my Tenth Step, because writing brought me to great discoveries about what I was experiencing beneath my intense reactions. I reach for: *"the feeling underneath the feeling",* so I can get to the core of the matter. For example, when I replaced my focus on the fear I was experiencing, to what I thought that fear was about, I was able to acknowledge my deep sadness in a particular situation. I was afraid to acknowledge that I had wanted to move on, but as a default, fear overtook me. It was well –worth the effort to sit with the uncomfortable experience, because the fear dissipated, much to my surprise. I also discovered that this step is enormously powerful for survivors, because you practice noticing what is going on inside of you (conscious contact), accepting responsibility (instead of controlling), identifying your truth, and owning your deeper feelings. It is the end of the road of suffering, for some survivors, who lived their whole lives pretending that their abusive experience did not occur, did not matter, or that their feelings are not legitimate.

Most survivors have issues with anger management. Some repress their anger, resulting in depression, anxiety, panic, passive-aggressive behavior, or covert aggression. Others lose control with inappropriate expressions of rage. Some of the consequences of poor anger management; include domestic violence, hostility, and untreated addictions. At the root of this anger, is the original experience of having been overpowered by someone or something that interrupted your life in a significantly harmful way.

If you were forced to lie about this experience, or if you were punished or rejected for having been a victim, there was no support to be real and honest. Under the threat of attack the normal instinct is to fight or run. Very often, and tragically, survivors did not have the opportunity to do either, and end up frozen instead. The result of this is suppressing anger, the very opposite of fighting back. You learn to hide, to lie, to blame, to project, and to run.

If you were a victim of abuse, you may live in a perpetual hide-and-seek chase with yourself. You create this desperate chase because you believe the lies about the abuse and doubt your own feelings and perceptions. You therefore cannot face the truth. The Tenth Step can help you to regain a truthful perspective about yourself. Do not ever be afraid that your particular experiences are too overwhelming for the Tenth Step to help you. You will be amazed at how this can empower you to learn how to shed your masks and layers, and live a life that reflects the Real You.

WHEN YOU WERE WRONG PROMPTLY ADMITTED IT

For the average ego-driven person, this part of Step Ten asks you to do something that is not a comfortable action. For survivors, this can trigger feelings or thoughts of "being bad" and therefore self-blaming. Admitting to when you are wrong clears away the confusion about your real role in upsetting situations. No one is ever always right or wrong, but when you are influenced by your dysfunctional beliefs, your sense of responsibility gets distorted and by tainted false beliefs.

Admission of wrongs also teaches you that you can have honest relationships with people, and you do not have to live a shamed-based life dictated by the effects of trauma. There may be instances where you were wronged, but instead of handling the situation appropriately, you sought revenge against the person. Although the incident started out with you being innocent of any wrongdoing (hence "right" in this situation), your actions are the "wrong" that needs to be admitted promptly. However, just like with the Ninth Step, you need to be cautious in admitting a wrong, lest it cause harm to someone else.

The Tenth Step inventory is a great gauge to monitor where you are in your recovery and spiritual growth. A word of caution: you are not wrong just because you have an emotional reaction, or because someone decides that you are wrong. Remember that feelings and emotions are never moral issues, and people are always going to have their opinions and judgments about it. **Step Ten is about being honest if you behaved in a way that you regret.** You need honesty for this spiritual practice of deep self-inquiry, especially if you are prone to ignoring your feelings or behaviors.

In my experience with the Tenth Step inventory, I learned that when I thought I was wrong and had to make amends, I was just avoiding strong feelings. It became easier for me to differentiate when I did not have to "own" anything except my feelings, and when I needed to set things right. It also became easier over time, to let go of the outcome. When I got myself in the habit of working through painful situations, I could see that in some cases, someone else "owns" the problem, and I could "own" my powerlessness over it.

Not every situation will afford the opportunity to do something constructive about it. For example, it is natural to feel tension if you disagree with your boss. Perhaps you discovered that you make better decisions than she does, and you are more sensitive when it comes to handling difficult issues in the workplace. Maybe your parents, in-laws, friends or neighbors, have declared war on you because you are setting healthy boundaries for the first time in your life, and they can no longer walk all over you. Regardless of the situation, if you have decided it is the right action to admit your wrong in the situation, like not setting healthy boundaries, apply the same caution that you have applied in the Ninth Step. Do not cause any harm with your admission of wrong-doing.

There may be situations where you become conscious that you hurt someone, although you may not know exactly what you did to hurt the person. If someone you care about has stopped speaking with you, you can make a general admission by stating: *"If I have hurt you in any way, please forgive me."* As an alternative, you can also approach the person and state that you seem to have noticed a shift in the relationship. Express that you care about the relationship and the person, and are available to listen to him. Encourage him to share his reaction or experience with you. The Tenth Step calls for personal reflection, which will come in handy when you cannot figure out what is your part in a changed attitude towards you. At times you will be able to achieve a mutual understanding, and at times the soundest solution is to walk away.

Before you go to sleep, constructively review your day. At the end of each day, write down one thing that went well and one thing that didn't. Then write the answer to the following question: *"What was my part in creating each of these situations?"* You keep yourself in reasonably good condition if you do it on a daily basis, rather than to wait until you are in crisis and have to dig yourself out of it. As I learned to become more truthful with myself utilizing my Tenth Step, I became less fearful and more confident. This created more meaningful and healthy connections. To my surprise, this kind of honesty and clarity prevents a lot of tension and drama. Over time and with practice, I have become less fearful of admitting if and when I am wrong. I learned that there is a clear difference between admitting a wrong and making amends, and being "less than" because I was wrong.

Admitting a wrong should not be a crushing experience, nor is its purpose to make you feel inferior in any way.

As long as I apply integrity to difficult situations, I have options. As long as my options reflect my truth and I have reached this truth by applying the spiritual principles, it is less likely that I will be attracted to unhealthy drama. Just as with everything worthwhile in life this takes practice, perseverance, self-discipline and integrity. If you are ready, come with me so we can explore Step Eleven.

"Paradise is not in repentance; Paradise is in the pure heart". [11]

---

[11] Gibran, Kahlil. *The Treasured Writings of Kahlil Gibran*, (New York: Castle Books, 2010), Pg. 814.

STEP ELEVEN

Sought through prayer and meditation to improve our conscious contact with God as we understood Him, praying only for knowledge of His will for us and the Power to carry that out.

Step Eleven is the daily practice and experience of deepening your awareness of your Higher Power through prayer and meditation. You are capable of prayer and meditation, regardless of your background or history. If you set aside the time daily, you can reach for whatever you believe is greater than, deeper than, or beyond yourself. Step Eleven also assumes that by now you have a conscious awareness of your Higher Power, and you are drawn to deepening that connection.

Think back to when you first started this journey, and you began to develop your conscious contact in Step Two.

Perhaps at the point of Step Two, you did not think you would have the capacity to trust this Transformative Power as you did in Step Three, or that you would reach for this Power throughout the steps. As you reflect back to your beginnings, you can see how effective prayer has been for you, and that with each heart-felt prayer, this connection has improved. If you were raised to believe that institutionalized prayer is "the only right way", know that your efforts to improve your conscious contact **as long as they reflect your personal spiritual path**, is the goal here.

Often spiritual seekers discover that their current spiritual practice does not feel the same as their childhood spiritual path. Some trauma survivors were raised in rigid religious systems that taught that God is punitive, disapproving, cold, distant, unloving, mysterious or distant. You may discover, through your application of the Twelve Steps to your trauma healing, that your experience with God is just the opposite:

forgiving, nurturing, understanding, loving, close, generous, and connected.

Transforming is about refining the human condition. Prayer and meditation can bring about a transformation you have not experienced before. Your spirituality will continue to change and evolve, as you deepen your connection to **your** Higher Power. The key is to remain open-minded so you can receive new ideas about yourself as a spiritual being having a human experience. You will have new insights about your fellow man, and the God who created us all.

It takes seeking through daily prayer and meditation to discover and understand personal truths. When you communicate with your Higher Power, you develop a new awareness of your connection with your Source of Life. It is a process of moving from how it is to how it could be. This communication is done through prayer and meditation. The work you did in Steps Three through Ten has allowed you to remove enough self-will that you can bring yourself to seek this "conscious contact".

Prayer and meditation is a departure from our usual way of functioning. We usually attempt to solve life's issues by using our five senses. In Step Eleven, you develop the ability to tap into a power greater than yourself beginning with five minutes of prayer and meditation in the morning, and five minutes in the evening. This is the simple way you *"establish conscious contact"* through utilizing a Sixth Sense. For most people, this is a sense that you may not even know you have, nor ever utilize. I was no different. When I first read this step, it seemed to be impossible for me to live a life of prayer and meditation. It seemed boring and confusing. I could not even sit quietly and still for five whole minutes. Like most people, I relied on logic, reason, knowledge and analysis. I did not trust that my prayers and meditation would have any effect on me, or connect me to the God I was seeking. However, the suggestions I learned in the Twelve Step rooms were both simple and powerful. I simply considered that I had a God who was personal to me, who cared about me as a person, and who would reveal to me whatever I needed to know at the time. I did not yet imagine that I had the gift of the Sixth Sense or that I would eventually receive the answers to questions I asked during meditation.

My willingness to establish "conscious contact" allowed me to begin by taking five minutes the first thing in the morning to sit in absolute quiet. I cleared my thoughts and listened to my breath. I asked my Higher Power to direct my thinking today, and to inspire my thoughts, decisions and intuitions. Daily, I pray for guidance so that when I go through the day, I am shown what my next step should be.

"God direct my thinking today so that it be divorced of self pity, dishonesty, self-will, self-seeking and fear. God inspire my thinking, decisions and intuitions. Help me to relax and take it easy. Free me from doubt and indecision. Guide me through this day and show me my next step. God give me what I need to take care of any problems. I ask all these things that I may be of maximum service to you and my fellow man in the name of the Steps I pray. AMEN"[12]

---

[12] *Alcoholics Anonymous*, 3rd edition, New York: Alcoholics Anonymous World Services, Inc., 1976. (The "Big Book."), Pg. 86.

If you pray daily to be guided into right action (Good Orderly Direction=G.O.D.) each morning, the chances are that your thoughts will be of much higher quality. I personally believe that a Higher Power is the source of all blessings, and if I continue to internalize this, there is an expansion of what I am capable of achieving during the day.

I once heard that your spiritual barometer is how you get along with your fellow man. Most people struggle with human relations, in some way. If you face indecision as to how to respond during the day, ask God (Good Orderly Direction) for an intuitive thought to guide you. Utilizing meditation and prayer, you do not need to struggle. You simply ask for guidance. It is an amazing experience to discover the power of humility when you recognize that you do not have a solution, and then tap into your Sixth Sense for direction.

Once you are in the habit of asking to be shown what each next step should be, you will discover that God's will for you is often *not* what *you* thought best for yourself. This is commonly discussed in Twelve Step meetings, usually with a sense of wonderment and gratitude. If you do not pray with the intent that God become your errand boy, but rather pray only for the knowledge and the Power to carry out God's will, **you see that God's will is always what is best for you. There are places that you cannot go unless God takes you there personally.** You need to feed your mind with healthy "food", since your mind is running your life. There are numerous books available for guidance in prayer and meditation. Enjoy educating yourself on this single, most potent tool for action and change.

A word of caution about praying for things **you want**, instead of God's **will for you**: If you pray for God's will for you and the power to carry that out, **instead of a monologue aimed**

in God's direction, you will create the space for God to guide you far beyond what you are capable of figuring out on your own. Your quality of life will be on a much higher plane of consciousness. This continues to be my experience. If you are truly living a life based on doing God's will, you will create a life for yourself that will extend beyond your wildest dreams. You can invite other people to pray with you, creating spiritual community. There is a saying that goes like this: *"People that pray together stay together"*. And since prayer has many positive effects, it is wonderful to share it with others.

Remember to pause during the day when you feel agitated or doubtful, and remind yourself that you are no longer running the show (Steps Two and Three). I promise you that this all really works. If you follow these suggestions, you will develop your own conscious contact, and it will have an amazing effect on your day-to-day challenges.

ROADBLOCKS TO MEDITATION AND PRAYER

Even though prayer and meditation is positive and rewarding, old habits die hard. If you are used to an uninterrupted mind of your own, you may not easily be up for a break from it. Sitting quietly for even one minute can seem very long. Take a moment right now, set your timer for one minute, and see how long it feels. In the beginning, your new practice may seem unnerving, especially if you are used to being busy and doing many things at once. However, the skill of being absolutely quiet goes beyond all other activities. You are harnessing the most powerful organ of any living thing: the human mind.

Perhaps when you see the words *"Sought through prayer and meditation"*, you feel uneasy about the solitary implication of the word "sought". You may be used to doing everything with someone else, and do not spend too much time alone, or in solitude. If that is the case, you can reframe this as: *"the practice that will help take my thinking to a different level."* Do you enjoy waking up every morning with the same worries, and the same troubling issues? We all need a break from the problems we have, and many problems originate in our thinking. Prayer and meditation helps you to achieve an absence of thinking certain thoughts, which leads you to serenity.

Your blockages to joyful living are created by thoughts that deprive you of serenity. When you ask to be directed in your thinking, and to be rid of certain thoughts, you will not magically be rid of all them at once. But this process helps you to enter an intuitive level, an inner level of guidance. Intuitive guidance operates within every person, all the time, and prayer (*asking*), and meditation (*listening*) accesses this power. My favorite analogy which I heard at a Twelve Step meeting is that your inner guidance is like a radio signal that can instruct you as to where you need to be going, doing, or thinking. Your regular thinking, unaided by prayer and meditation, is the radio static. If you can hear the whole message clearly, without the static, you receive both a positive signal *and* clear direction. **You do not need to search for this Positive Guiding Signal outside yourself, because it is available inside you all the time. The static blocks your ability to hear and comprehend what it is trying to communicate to you.** This explanation of "conscious contact" resonates so clearly with me.

If you can use the techniques of prayer and meditation to get in touch with the reality that everything is fine, and that you are being taken care of, you have clearly heard the voice of the Positive Guiding Signal speaking to you. I encourage you to take a leap of faith, and see if prayer takes your thinking to this higher level.

TRY IT OUT!

I would like to suggest that you now take some time to read your favorite prayer, scripture, poem, or passage, whatever the topic or source. Consider that the words on the page are written thoughts that would not come naturally to most of us. Read them aloud, and ask yourself if these are thoughts that would naturally come to your mind. The person who wrote them, I am sure, had to make time and space for such an activity, because it requires that a person access a deeper part of themselves. For me, writing this book is a constant practice and reminder of going deeper. To be inspired, all you need is to set aside time daily to have your thoughts be deeply guided. Undoubtedly, this type of activity generates huge rewards that are practical, supportive, and uplifting. But you have to experience it for yourself.

If you have been raised with formalized prayer, you may doubt that a God, who is personal to you, wants you pray. This is a common issue and an unfortunate roadblock. Personally, I have experienced this impediment for a long time. Although there are no quick and easy answers, my experiences taught me that the way to establish *conscious contact* is through my heart.

There were periods in my life when praying and meditating felt like a huge sacrifice, because of how blocked and confused I felt. I did not give up, and kept on practicing Step 11. Over time, and with patience, I found that prayer went from feeling like a sacrifice to an experience that drew me near to my Inner Guide. It brought me full circle, from a place of disconnect and isolation, to a life shaped by this "conscious contact". When you are in meditation and prayer, allow your heart to be involved in a process of self surrender. Become open to this "Sixth Sense". Trust that this process will eventually become a bridge between your human mind, through your Soul (True Self), and to God. **What occurs on this bridge is a free flowing exchange, the makings of a deep relationship with God.**

IDENTIFYING GOD'S WILL

A very common question I have had for myself, and I have heard others discuss, is how exactly do you know what is God's will for you? Since you pray in Step Eleven *"only for knowledge of His will for us and the Power to carry that out"*, do I have to be at a certain level of spirituality to receive and interpret this information? The simplest answer which I live by, is that I am doing "God's will," **when I am aware, and I respond appropriately**. This means being willing to let go of controlling that which is not in my Power to control, **and it also means acting responsibly when I am challenged**.

One common misconception about doing "God's will" is that it is a passive, non-reactive stance, regardless of the circumstances. By surrendering unconditionally, you may not be speaking up when you need to. It is always God's will for you to respond with the "next right action". Sometimes that means that you need to take a stand for yourself or for someone else. You may need to not respond to someone pressuring you. You may be called to champion something that is close to your heart. I have had times in my life, where I was challenged to simply allow others their reactions, however unpleasant it was for me. In those moments, God's will for me was to not react. In other circumstances, it was the appropriate action for me to speak up and advocate for my needs. If the other person could not respond, I could peacefully walk away without insisting that they change.

The overall feeling of living a life based on God's will for me is an experience of centeredness and trust in the midst of the storm. **It is not an absence of certain thoughts, feelings, or beliefs, but a sense of cooperating with a Spirit Greater than me.** I also carry with me, a belief that I am a spiritual being having a human experience. I do not fully understand what this means, or how exactly I am connected to God and others. For today, I do not need to figure it all out. I am much more comforted practicing and praying, and responding in ways that serve my growth. This gives me joy knowing that I am aligned with my Higher Power. When I am so aligned, conflicts resolve very differently than if I were unaligned.

THE POWER TO CARRY THAT OUT

The second part of Step Eleven is praying for the power to carry out that knowledge of God's will for you, once you are aware of what that knowledge may be. The word "power" includes a variety of qualities including: patience, perseverance, honesty, humility, and compassion. It does not refer to "power" in the typical sense that you may think of it. Inner power is not "power over" another like force, coercion, control, or domination over others. It is in fact, opposite of what you may normally apply to situations, when you think you need to accomplish something spectacular. The power to carry out God's will requires you to be assertive, apply a sense of justice, eagerness, caution, courage, and a sense of humor.

These qualities may not be in your comfort zone of a "power-display", especially when there is ongoing pressure to live your life according to society or your family's will for you. You may actually find yourself lacking support from society or family to live your life according to God's will. You receive neither their approval nor guidance for the power to carry that out. So this step may have you really question its validity, and may push you out of your comfort zone. And yet, when you begin focusing on a higher purpose above and beyond yourself, you will experience less fear and more satisfaction with your life. Serenity is one of the gifts of Step Eleven.

Through prayer and meditation, I have greatly lessened my need to control other people. I have significantly opened myself to receiving miracles, blessings, and gifts in all forms. I could never have achieved this without a regular spiritual practice. *"There is a direct linkage among self-examination, meditation, and prayer. Taken separately, these practices can bring much relief and benefit. But when they are logically related and interwoven, they result in an unshakable foundation for life."* [13]

FOUR QUESTIONS FOR REFLECTION

---

[13] *Twelve Steps and Twelve Traditions*, New York: Alcoholics Anonymous World Services, Inc., 1981. (The "Twelve and Twelve.") Pg. 98

1. How does my current understanding of my Creator, compare with the understanding I had when I started this process in Step One?

_____

_____

_____

_____

2. Have I made a list of the qualities that my Creator has, and do any of those qualities have transformative power for me personally?

_____

_____

_____

_____

3. From my personal life experiences, how would I describe my Higher Power?

_____

_____

_____

_____

4. From my answers, what is my understanding of God right now?

_____

_____

_____

_____

"The heart's affections are divided like the branches of the cedar tree; if the tree loses one strong branch, it will suffer but it does not die. It will pour all its vitality into the next branch so that it will grow and fill the empty place." [14]

---

[14] Gibran, Kahlil. *The Treasured Writings of Kahlil Gibran*, (New York: Castle Books, 2010), Pg. 834.

STEP TWELVE

Having had a spiritual awakening as the result of these steps, we tried to carry this message to alcoholics and to practice these principles in all our affairs.

You start your recovery process with identifying, and relating to a Higher Power as *you* understand this Power. This understanding, in partnership with applying time-tested principles, puts you in touch with that power greater than yourself. As you continue to apply the principles, and your understanding deepens, you can explain to yourself what this Power is, and how it manifests in your personal life journey.

At this point, you have experienced a spiritual awakening personal to you. This has happened slowly and gradually, as you have been patiently working the steps. If you have been asleep for a long period of time, you may need a long period of time to awaken. It does not happen overnight. Step

Twelve is about having experienced a deep and effective spiritual experience. For you, that may mean that you feel changes in your life that you can attribute to something spiritual. There are those people for whom a spiritual awakening is about expanding their understanding of true honesty, and then living accordingly. Each spiritual principle that is connected to the Twelve Steps will contribute to your spiritual awakening, as you are willing to deepen your experience.

Let us take a look at the meaning of "spiritual awakenings". Take a moment now to write down your understanding of this term and how it compares to the definition that you self-identified in the first chapter.

_____

_____

_____

_____

Trauma and Transformation: A 12-Step Guide.

_____

_____

You may have experienced a single spiritual awakening, or a series of awakenings. For example, it might be when you first learned to say "yes" when you mean "yes", and say "no" when you mean "no". This is evidenced by learning about healthy boundaries, and setting them appropriately. As a result, you know how to not allow people to take advantage of you, and how to not take advantage of them. As you awaken, you become aware of your mind-body-soul connection. You pay attention to the inner messages you receive, and speak up for yourself, having once been so afraid to do so. You stop trying to control others, or allowing yourself to be controlled or manipulated. All these are examples of a *"spiritual awakening"*, which can resolve the typical struggles for survivors of trauma.

In its simplest form, a *"spiritual awakening"* includes anything that relates to becoming more awake, more present, more self-aware, and more self-supporting. Some people refer to this as a "psychic change", or a shift in perception. It does not matter what you personally call it. Awakenings happen, slowly, over time, and are different from a *"spiritual experience"* which happens suddenly. Since your personality developed over time, your awakening happens over time as well.

This psychic change/spiritual awakening does not happen in your life without connecting to a Power greater than yourself. This connection is the essence of a spiritual experience. If you still do not believe that such a power exists, review what you have achieved in your life until this point. Review all the beliefs and knowledge you had prior to starting the Twelve Steps, and compare it to what you know at this point. Take a few moments now to write your beliefs about a Higher Power (after having applied steps one through eleven). How can your current understanding of your Higher Power help you work through and heal from the results of your traumatic experience(s)? Is there a difference between what you know now, in comparison to when you first began your journey? Can you see the role and value of an open mind when it comes to changing what you want to change in your life?

TIP:

Change is a key word in exploring the subject of spiritual experience.

Conceptualizing the Personal Relationship in Spiritual Healing

Write your **beliefs** about a Higher Power (after having applied steps one through eleven).	How can your **current understanding** of your Higher Power help you work through and heal from the results of your traumatic experience(s)?	Is there a **difference** between what you know *now*, in comparison to when you first began your journey?	Can you see the role and value of an **open mind** when it comes to changing what you want to change in your life?

Trauma and Transformation: A 12-Step Guide.

In your personal work on Steps One through Eleven, you have been expanding your thoughts, feelings, and behaviors, replacing what are outdated and incorrect, with truth, tenderness, and transformative beliefs. The Twelfth Step is about a life awakening from your own psychic sleep. It is about a life of being connected to your Inner Self, your Higher Power, or whatever you choose to call "God". You have awakened to something far deeper and greater than your own stand-alone resources, ideas, strengths, and self-will. This is an emotional re-arrangement because you now experience peace of mind, and subsequently a new willingness to help other people.

I firmly believe that the deepest change comes through spirituality (a caring, personal relationship with your Higher Power, safe others, and living a life guided by principles that promote goodness, truth, kindness, and forgiveness). This change we are discussing *is not about being someone you are not.* It is about taking a look at how you have arrived to be the person you are, as influenced by your traumatic experiences, and reaching to become what your' Creator intended for you to be. For example, if you are a highly creative person and were shamed in childhood, you may not be living a life utilizing your creative gifts. Fear and shame-based thinking is the great inhibitor. A part of your recovery will be to uncover this gift, get to know it, and put it to work for a good cause! Take time now to examine what you would be if you reached for the gifts you were endowed with, and fearlessly brought them to life.

_____

_____

_____

_____

Having emotional reasons to not live out your true potential is a huge emotional displacement. You may have gone your whole life believing that the way you are is set in stone, only to find out that it was an effect, and not the real definition of you. Many trauma survivors feel as if they are broken into pieces that do not fit together. They describe feeling split inside, where their thoughts, feelings, and behaviors do not quite feel right, or belong to them. Perhaps you feel confused or ashamed at the intensity of your anger, pain, chronic feeling of emptiness or disconnect from life and people in general. You may feel that, in some significant way which you do not quite understand, your life has been out of control. You may take a look at Step Twelve as it relates the first eleven steps, and not see how any of this will accomplish the goal of having a spiritual awakening as it pertains to you and your survival of trauma.

Since trauma is about significant loss, disruption, and disconnect, this journey back to yourself and to your Higher Power, will determine the depth of your healing on an emotional level. This does not mean that you will never again experience the range of human emotions and frailties. You will feel whatever difficult emotions you experience time and time again. This journey is not about eradicating your humanness, or never feeling anger or despair. What you will gain is a deeper and more spiritually attuned understanding of yourself. This attunement will extend throughout your three-fold system: mind, body and soul - since trauma affects all three. Spiritually-based trauma recovery occurs when there is a transformation, and a dispelling, of the pent – up energy and toxicity that has collected inside. You will accept when you are powerless, ask for help instead of isolating, and recognize that things are becoming different and better. You commit to acting in the right way, even if you do not have the feelings to do so.

> **TIP:**
>
> If you are unsure of the right action to take, think of the character defect that informs your typical response. Then choose its opposite!

Your entire journey through the Twelve Steps is to bring you to Step Twelve when you awaken to and connect with your Spirit. You may feel less bitter and angry, less frightened and confused, no longer lost and depressed. You may experience many more moments of happiness, joy, and freedom. You still have some of the same problems you once had, but you feel happy and positive, for reasons you cannot fully explain. **Since you have no outside reasons for change in attitude, you can safely attribute this to a change that took place inside of you. This is "healing".**

In hindsight, you can see how these eleven steps have helped you to prepare for the gift of awakening to what is really going on. And what is really on is that you are a Spiritual Being having a human experience. Due to your suffering, you remained unaware and disconnected from this simple and profound truth. However, now you can apply courage and discipline with all that you have learned to stop a difficult moment, from eliminating behavioral patterns that escalate out of your control, and from living in hiding.

TIP:

Preparing yourself to receive this wondrous gift requires the admiration and desire for it.

In order for you to receive mail, you need to put up a mailbox that is the correct size, placed in the correct location, with your name and address on it. If you do not have the appropriate container or desire to receive mail, the post office will not deliver your mail to you. If you did not set up a mailbox, would you claim that you never get any mail, or that no one ever thinks of you or writes to you? "Why does everyone else get mail, but not me?" If you close yourself off spirituality, you are missing the support and structure to receive this gift. This may then cause you to feel that a Higher Power does not in fact exist, and that you just *"don't get it, but everyone else does".*

When you utilize these Twelve Steps of Alcoholics Anonymous to unblock your awareness of a Higher Power, your pain will lessen. **Without having a spiritual awakening you may misdiagnose what is missing.** Surviving trauma often creates a perpetual feeling of void. You may assume that if you acquire worldly possessions such as money, relationships, or lovers that your pain will disappear. **When this is your solution to fill your inner void, you are misdiagnosing your pain. What is missing is a genuine connection with your Higher Self.** This missing connection is what creates the feelings of emptiness and sense of disconnect. The proof of this is seen in people who have impressive materialistic achievements, and still complain of that chronic void. The solution is to address what is really missing by applying the ancient, time-tested, and potent spiritual principles upon which the Twelve Steps of Alcoholics Anonymous are based. This spiritual growth will nurture your capacity to experience this connection.

Most people cannot change the consequences of their particular wounding on their own. The constellation of defenses and adaptive behaviors, require the appropriate interventions and support. In order to affect a spiritual awakening, a person requires a deep, genuine desire for it.

Nurturing this involves ridding yourself of attitudes, beliefs and behaviors that are self-destructive. It also involves pursuing the truth, correct information, and just enough trust to be devoted to your healing. There is no quick-fix.

CARRYING THE MESSAGE

You "carry the message" when you share your own experience with another person who is seeking your support for a similar situation. The message is that you have found a Higher Power that is personal to you, and you share your belief that this Power helps you when you are honest, open, and willing. This is a humble sharing and you do not have to understand how it works, or be an expert. You simply remain honest, open, and willing *enough* to take the necessary action with each of the Twelve Steps. The tone is one of compassionate sharing of what has helped you, **not** a form of religious prothletising.

Some trauma survivors feel too badly damaged to believe that they can get well. These steps are used to reveal your potential for trauma-recovery. Remember that "potential" refers to something that has not yet happened, and that you have to work for your potential to come alive. If you take the Twelve Steps, one by one, patiently and faithfully, you are getting caught up in the Spiritual Solution. You have begun to live a new way of life.

The first step to starting a new way of life is to acknowledge where you are in this moment. Right now *"you are exactly where you are meant to be"*. In social work we say: *"start where the client is at."* They mean the same thing: start from the exact point where you are now. Acknowledge the areas in which you struggle, and the areas where you succeed. You may feel that you do not have anything to offer someone else, or perhaps the opposite tendency to want to fix other people, or give unsolicited advice. Do not do that; simply share your own personal experience, strength and hope so that you can invite others to do the same for themselves.

Working with other people, when you are healed enough, may become a very important part of your life. If you support people in getting the necessary help and are there to simply share your experience, strength, and hope, you may bear witness to someone getting better. Never share what you do not know, or what you do not have the capacity for. **You can help another survivor by simply supporting them in getting the help they need.** If you are unable to do anything further, it is enough to get someone started on *their* personal journey.

BECOMING THE MESSENGER

There is tremendous power in being a messenger of good in someone else's life. When you experience your own personal transformation, you will naturally want to influence other people to experience the same kind of release and change. This desire to carry the message stems from your having been so lost in your personal suffering, and then turning the most painful and dark parts of your past into a special gift to pass on. **If you have prepared yourself appropriately, the person you pass it on to will connect with that part of you that genuinely transformed.** If you had a terrible past and yet you choose to seek recovery and treatment, you can share with others how you have genuinely gone from "darkness to light".

However, in order to be a Messenger, it must be the Real You that is doing the carrying, and delivering, of the Message. Most people begin their Twelve Step journey not knowing who they really are, and maybe living from their False Self. However, by the time you reach Step Twelve, you may realize that the person you thought you were at the start of your journey is not at all who you really are. This Real You that has emerged is the one that is carrying and delivering the message. This may be the first time in your life that you are genuinely reaching out to other people. Perhaps this is the first time where you realize that everything you have been told about yourself, and everything you have believed about yourself, is not true at all. Certain traumatic effects operate just like that. Examples include: poor self-esteem and self-worth, a core belief of being bad and unworthy, or a sense of being helpless and useless.

Each trauma survivor has personal, intimate knowledge of the long, dark night of this process of revelation. Many of you have walked through this long night as you try to reconcile your traumatic history and how it may have shattered you. For some of you, this journey has afforded you the experience of deep awareness of what it means to be the recipient of the love and guidance from human "angels".

No one is able to heal in isolation. With the assistance of your unique angels along the way, you come to see that you have been created in the Divine Image "... a*nd it was good*". Angels can appear as beloved friends who light up your path, by being true to their own path. You are nourished by kindness, love, and generosity, regardless of what form and voice your angel takes. One of my personal angels is my gift of the Sixth Sense. This gift from God deepens along with my desire to have this direct access to my Creator.

In Exodus 23:20-25, the discussion centers on an Angel who will "***guard you on the way and bring you to the place that I have prepared***". What exactly is this place that God has prepared? The personalized answer is the unique circle where only I and my Creator can stand together. <u>This is the most intimate space, and in it, I acknowledge that everything that I am is God's gift to me, and what I do with my life, is my gift back to God.</u> There is no one that can stand in this exact circle with me, and I have received a lot of assistance from angels to help me get to this place.

To travel along this path, and to have moments where I feel myself standing in This Circle, is to have enough courage, trust, vulnerability, and awareness that I am not alone. I share this journey of mine to pass along the message that each person's path is ultimately to reach this intimate space with their Creator. You can achieve this no matter what you survived. This is why the verse states that the Angel will guard YOU and bring you on THE way, and bring you to THE place that G-d has prepared. THE path is a universal arrival place of Oneness with All There Is. It is unique and universal at the same time.

The verses caution you to *"Pay attention to this angels' presence and listen to its' voice."* To ask you to pay attention, listen, be mindful and aware, can be an enormous challenge if you had to remain numb in order to survive. However, you deserve this ultimate connection. Dedicate time every day to let your angel know that you have arrived at a still point and are ready to listen. In this way, you introduce and open yourself to encountering different Messengers along the way. Such Messengers are placed in your path, because you need them. Perhaps they train you to be an angel for other people. Life has many difficulties, challenges, and painful aspects as well as joy, creativity, and enlightenment. We are designed to have a spiritual experience. Inherent in this reality is the summation of our relationship with God as an intensely personal and protective one.

If you are one of those trauma survivors who do not believe you have the potential to be a loving, giving, open, and happy person, due to your wounds, I urge you to evaluate where this voice is coming from. Your ego will always want you to believe that you are a Separate Self and that you are stuck and set in the way that you are forever. There is a wonderful joy in applying spiritual principles, and discovering that maybe you are not that stuck after all. You do not need to live with such hopelessness. You do not need to live a limited life due to events that were out of your control.

Most internal suffering is about the difference between who you really are, and what others told you about yourself. I arrived at this insight when I realized just how many trauma survivors are held back from discovering and exploring meaning in life. Part of this reason is because they were given certain messages that became embedded in their psyche, but were designed by God in a totally different way. As you can imagine, it is difficult to seek and pursue a meaningful life carrying this raging internal battle. Think about it, and think about all the unnecessary conflict and suffering you have right now in this moment. Does any of this suffering have to do with you being blocked by old self-limiting ideas? When you are exposed to the Twelve Steps, you are facing a potential mirror. Through this diligent process, your False Self will be less and less necessary, and eventually completely obsolete. This will cause all kinds of wonderful things to occur as you manifest your true potential.

PRACTICING THESE PRINCIPLES IN ALL OUR AFFAIRS...

When you practice anything in life, you become better at it, less intimidated by it, and more confident. Practicing spiritual principles in all your affairs is no different. As you become more familiar with your personal challenges, you develop the ease and confidence of applying spiritual principles in order to meet such challenges. You know a place to go for help with your difficulties. Certain effects of trauma can be very immobilizing. Intense fear responses, very common for survivors, lessen over time given the right interventions. Although the triggers may always be there inside you, the application of spiritual principles can influence your viewpoint, so that your triggers and difficulties will take on a different meaning.

When you accept and integrate the Twelve Steps, you move into a space of strength and pro-active confidence. This is because you achieve an inner place of balance and understanding that may be completely new. It is not the same place of emptiness, confusion, and unmanageability. For each survivor, this spiritual awakening is a different experience, and **it is reflective of each person's unique spiritual path**. No two people have the same spiritual path, and therefore no two survivors will experience healing the same way. However, if you apply the Twelve Steps with honesty, openness, and willingness (H.O.W.), you will awaken in ways you cannot imagine.

MY OWN PERSONAL AWAKENING

I experienced a series of spiritual awakenings, and I believe that I will continue to awaken throughout my life. As part of this process, I saw clearly that I could not change the facts of the traumatic events that took place in my life, and by whom I was betrayed, but that I *could choose* different responses to old triggers. I also had a new interpretation of past events, and after considerable dedicated involvement in my recovery, **was able to separate human self-will from the will of God**. My understanding, and therefore relationship, with my Higher Power evolved significantly over time. This understanding and soul-level acceptance had a great effect as it reached into my internal trauma-pockets, for healing and comfort.

I also awakened my willingness to let go of unhealthy people, places, and things, and to embrace love and change. I now feel a greater sense of serenity and self-acceptance. I have had flashes of enlightenment, and prolonged experiences of clarity, confidence, and strength. *I learned how to turn within and listen to the angel inside who speaks in gentle whispers.* Such spiritual awakenings changed my life.

My awakening was also a physical one. The particulars of my trauma history are tragic, as all traumatic events are. One of my ways of coping was to shut down physically. I experienced mostly being numb and out of touch with my body. This defensive numbness is a common trauma reaction, often employed in order to survive pain. I felt like my body was asleep most of the time. I had little awareness or knowledge of my sensations, feelings, and needs. I was surprised that applying spiritual principles of the Twelve Steps of Alcoholics Anonymous helped me come back to life in my heart. This experience eventually led me to be interested in healing my own body. I am grateful for the process of becoming more aware of what is going on inside of me. My curiosity took me to further explore emotions gets stored in the body. This is the most unexpected spiritual awakening.

I have experienced a spiritual awakening on all levels of my being. It is a deeper sense of self-discovery and self-connection. Because of this, I experience life much more fully: physically, emotionally, and mentally. I enjoy life to the degree that I feel spiritually connected, and I believe that this can be achieved for other survivors as well. Remember that trauma can have effects that sever the connection between the mind, body, and soul, the relationship that I call: **The Holy Triangle.**

This process of recovery and spirituality is about becoming who *you* were meant to be, despite whatever you survived, at what age you survived it, and what you lack or are in possession of: physically, emotionally, and spiritually. It is well worth making the effort to inquire who you really are, and then discovering that through your True Self you are connected to everything else. If you are beginning to awaken to this truth, you have begun to awaken to the deepest reality of all living things: that life means that we are all connected on some deep, mysterious level of existence.

TIPS FOR CARRYING THE MESSAGE

If you are approached by a trauma survivor who is seeking healing, the following are some guidelines to help you carry the message of recovery and healing.

1) ONLY if you do not feel obligated to do so, **describe** your personal experience with recovery and growth. In the Big Book of Alcoholics Anonymous it gives you clear direction

that you share: *"what you used to be like, what happened, and what you are like now."* [15]

2) Listen, empathize and encourage the survivor to seek whatever help is necessary.

3) Use discretion to decide how you carry the message. If what you are sharing is based on having looked deeply into your own story, the message should reflect your personal spiritual path.

4) Refrain from telling someone what to do, or giving unsolicited advice. This can be perceived as criticism. Instead, offer a suggestion, and accepted, share your observations, and personal experiences of recovery.

---

[15] *Alcoholics Anonymous*, 3rd edition, New York: Alcoholics Anonymous World Services, Inc., 1976. (The "Big Book.") Pg. 164

Trauma and Transformation: A 12-Step Guide.

5) Be mindful of getting too involved in other people's recovery. It is not healthy for either of you, and may be disguised as a defensive mechanism of escape and avoidance of your own issues that you need to be attending to.

6) You cannot give something away that you do not have. Do not skip over your personal work, and rush into helping others. To inspect what you have to give away, answer the following questions:

    a) Do I have the serenity "to know the difference" between what I can, and cannot control?

    _____

    _____

    b) Have I thoroughly explored my faith?

    _____

    _____

c) Have I conducted a searching, thorough, and honest review of my resentments, and behavioral patterns?

_____

_____

d) What are my expectations in reaching out to this person? Can I really share my own experience, and then be available to just listen, empathize, and let go of the outcome?

_____

_____

e) What are the indicators that this person is ready to hear the message I carry?

_____

_____

f) Do I need to seek wise counsel before approaching this person? Trust your gut instinct.

_____

_____

Remember: Discussing trauma and recovery is a highly sensitive and personal subject. Only share with others if you feel safe and trusting with the person. Do not do anything out of fear, guilt, or shame. Don't rush into anything.

...IN ALL OUR AFFAIRS

Practicing Step Twelve is about letting go of your old, dysfunctional way of relating. It is also about sharing your transformation which includes no longer being false, in hiding, or on the run. You will simply be your own genuine self. When you look in the mirror of other people, you will see a person who is real and true to their Spirit. This does not mean you have to be perfect, or know the answer to every question, for every circumstance, that comes up. You get to be your same imperfect self, but now you have an increased awareness and the help of the principles of the Twelve Step program to apply to every area of your life. We say in the program: "It works – if **YOU** work ***it***". This means that you make it a top priority to monitor your spiritual condition. When you regularly evaluation your spiritual condition, you will find that the areas of your life affected by trauma will improve.

> **FINAL TIP:**
>
> The transformation that occurs from practicing these principles in all your affairs, includes affecting those places inside you that were once broken. Through spiritual transformation, those once-broken places become the windows where the light of God shines through.

Thank you for reading this book! With the greatest sincerity and passion, I believe that if you apply yourself with an honest heart and the direction of a Higher Power, transforming your trauma will happen for you in due time. This is because the power of spirituality is all yours, is right here *for you,* **and best of all it works if you work it!** When you are on a spiritual path, in essence, you are headed in the same direction that your Higher Power is going. This is because, as the Talmud says: *"wherever a person wants to go they lead him"*. "They" refers to spiritual beings and the spiritual powers that be. Such a life of alignment with your Higher Power is a life that is vastly different from one where you are not aligned within your spiritual path. This is especially true for trauma survivors, who already have so much experience feeling misaligned and out of touch. It is no secret that life is not always easy or comfortable.

You struggle with so many issues by just being alive, and you have many unanswered questions. It is easy to just stay as you always were, and not bother to do what these steps call you to do: **1) search, 2) seek, 3) question, 4) examine, 5) make decisions, 6) amend your behaviors, and 7) seek a spiritual solution.** But the life of a person, who has been traumatized, and unhealed, is a lonely, disconnected life. If you do not have your own concept of a loving Higher Power, you are welcome to borrow mine. Hold on to it until you develop your own. And be prepared, when the time is right, to lend your concept of a loving Higher Power to the next survivor who has not yet formulated their own.

Remember that the mind and body had to shut down and hide in order to survive. Therefore, connection on all levels is the linchpin of genuine recovery. If you go off track, do not worry. Getting back on track is simple, and involves taking small steps, consistently and patiently.

I hope that in sharing my own experience of strength and hope throughout this book, that I have been a faithful carrier of this powerful message to even one trauma survivor. If I reached inside you and touched you, it is my hope that you have been awakened, even for just a moment. Perhaps that moment will be the ship that takes you to the unchartered territory within yourself...that place where the treasure chests have been buried and long-forgotten.

> *"Life without freedom is like a body without a soul, and Freedom without Thought is like a confused spirit....Life, Freedom, and Thought are three-in-one, and are everlasting and never pass away."* [16]

---

[16] Gibran, Kahlil. *The Treasured Writings of Kahlil Gibran*, (New York: Castle Books, 2010), Pg. 834.

Trauma and Transformation: A 12-Step Guide.

The Twelve Steps of Alcoholics Anonymous

1. We admitted we were powerless over alcohol - that our lives had become unmanageable.

2. Came to believe that a Power greater than ourselves could restore us to sanity.

3. Made a decision to turn our will and our lives over to the care of God as we understood Him.

4. Made a searching and fearless moral inventory of ourselves.

5. Admitted to God, to ourselves and to another human being the exact nature of our wrongs.

6. Were entirely ready to have God remove all these defects of character.

7. Humbly asked Him to remove our shortcomings.

8. Made a list of all persons we had harmed, and became willing to make amends to them all.

9. Made direct amends to such people wherever possible, except when to do so would injure them or others.

10. Continued to take personal inventory and when we were wrong promptly admitted it.

11. Sought through prayer and meditation to improve our conscious contact with God as we understood Him, praying only for knowledge of His will for us and the power to carry that out.

12. Having had a spiritual awakening as the result of these steps, we tried to carry this message to alcoholics and to practice these principles in all our affairs.[17]

The Twelve Steps are reprinted with permission of Alcoholics Anonymous World Services, Inc. ("AAWS") Permission to reprint the Twelve Steps does not mean that AAWS has reviewed or approved the contents of this publication, or that AAWS necessarily agrees with the views expressed herein. A.A. is a program of recovery from alcoholism only - use of the Twelve Steps in connection with programs and activities which are patterned after A.A., but which address other problems, or in any other non-A.A. context, does not imply otherwise.

[17] *Alcoholics Anonymous*, 3rd edition, New York: Alcoholics Anonymous World Services, Inc., 1976. (The "Big Book."), 59-60

AFTERWARD

WHAT TO DO WITH THE PAIN OF P.T.S.D.

"You were born with wings, why prefer to crawl through life?"

-Rumi

"There is a candle in your heart, ready to be kindled. There is a void in your soul, ready to be filled. You feel it, don't you?"

-Rumi

"The wound is the place where the Light enters you."

-Rumi

SOUL-PAIN

Pain is a response, an internal expression of your hurt and wound. Pain can be hidden and create a silent suffering that no one knows but the survivor. Pain can also be revealed by the survivor in ways in which they respond to having their pained activated. All people have a deep desire to be loved and cared for, and survivors are no different. Often times chronic, debilitating pain means that the survivor has not appropriately processed what originally caused, or causing, their pain. Some survivors may be aware of their pain-blockages and can experience intense sadness and anger by their inability to do anything about it. Because of this, the lives of some survivors are lacking in warm, close bonds or a stable social network.

The histories of those survivors that experience chronic pain are typically characterized by traumatic experiences, severe enough to create a crater-in-the-soul. This soul-crater is that part of you that feels like an empty dark place, cold, alienated, and all alone. This is your 'personal pain pocket'. While there are numerous effective tools, techniques and psychotherapies available in the field of mental health, a survivor's pain-pocket(s) can go untouched and unhealed for a variety of reasons. Because of their intense, ongoing pain, a survivor may feel that they are prisoners of their bodies and trapped by simply being alive. Some of these survivors are high functioning individuals, who go through life hiding their invisible wound, some function below optimal level, and there are those that make their pain obvious in highly destructive ways.

Regardless of a survivor's outward appearance, inside, survivors that suffer with chronic emotional pain feel inferior to others and suspect that they are stigmatized for carrying such a heavy wound. Despite some survivors' being adapted to their environment or even highly successful, they feel they have to carefully conceal the nature and extent of their hurt because they will be rejected by others. This puts survivors in a predicament: participate in life and keep their true suffering and struggles hidden, or reveal their pain and hurt and risk being rejected. Some survivors are unable to experience the friendship and love that they witness others experiencing, and they are left to wonder what, if anything, they have to really live for.

Survivors who live with this kind of often-hidden pain suffer beyond words. This is obvious. Deep pain causes deep suffering. People deal with it in their own ways; sometimes they choose to seek healing and healthy expression, and sometimes they bury, deny it, and seek to numb it out. But most unhealthy methods of denying and numbing the pain only end in disillusionment due to the mind, body, and soul that are always seeking healing. At some point, a survivor may feel discouraged by their failure to remain numb and blind to their pain, and are confronted by their vulnerability when they least expect it. Even though they try to change, the power of the pain and hurt, the fear of exposing their vulnerability, and the habit of thought that accompanies their coping style, leaves them stuck.

It is therefore extremely important to honor and recognize such lonely, hidden, suffering, and the accompanying piercing pain and vulnerability. This is not to be ignored. A lack of such acknowledgement renders a discussion of a trauma survivor incomplete.

However, there is another critical aspect to a survivor's pain that requires careful consideration and which I will explore in this final chapter. It is the aspect of pain that a survivor *does* have control over, and that is their thought-process. Knowing which untrue thoughts fuel his pain, takes the survivor's pain beyond a hopeless state of affairs, to a more hopeful, positive, and growth-oriented adventure.

There are certain characteristics of intense emotional pain, which are important to discuss here. Pain, without any influence upon it, lacks the power or wisdom to shift. The original pain is stimulated by triggers, memories, additional pain, needs, unrequited longings, desire, and basic human instincts. Sometimes the pain is intensified by long-term conditioning in coping with the pain. For some survivors, their coping method of choice is by freezing the pain out of their awareness, where it lingers in the outer-space of consciousness, stuck in a dark, timeless void-unreachable by anyone, not even himself. This survivor has part of them that exists in a state of lethargic sleep. He cannot move forward in life until someone comes along and awakens him.

Alternatively, some survivors, when they are faced with the winds of past painful memories blowing forcibly in different directions, will follow whichever wind is the most intense. This can manifest as impulsivity, compulsive-acting out, various modes of aggression, poor self-care, and various addictions to numb the pain, and other destructive means; all to tell their story. The intensity of the pain leaves little room for choosing healthy thoughts and actions, and can be blinding. When a survivor responds as such, they are devoid of strength and counsel. Their resistance is based on seeking instant gratification, instead of experiencing the awakening that accompanies being in touch with themselves and expressing grief. When the pain is awakened, it is critical to have access to it. As the saying goes *"If you can feel it, you can heal it."*

You, the survivor, may feel that when you are in activation-mode, you do not have a choice of free will in the moment. The brush of pain can make you feel like you are being suffocated inside of an erupted volcano. The negative consequence of not believing that **you do have a choice in how you deal with your pain** is to go to the opposite extreme. Tragically, this leads to compromised lives, not seeking meaningful pursuits, and indulging in various addictions and compulsions, including victim-blaming. It is sad when a survivor does not take care of themselves, or continually conditions to hurt themselves or others. This keeps remnants of the original trauma active, and perpetuates a legacy of shame, pain, and self-blame. If you are seeking to heal your pain, it may benefit you to be acquainted with the both the benefits of getting well, and the challenges that are part of the recovery process. I have laid them out clearly and extensively throughout this book.

THE CASE FOR TRAUMA-TRIGGER HEALING

It is my personal belief and faith that we are all here on earth to love, learn, do service, enjoy our beautiful planet, and each other. However, when you feel consistently trapped by suffocating pain, life is experienced as riding in an old, rickety, rusty open-car train, uphill, and going nowhere slowly. Existence can seem pointless, and you wander aimlessly through life feeling stuck and uncomfortable in your own body, without any relief in sight. You feel you have no control, and are just living to survive or numb out your pain. However, **by treating your pain responsibly**, a subject theme throughout this book, you will think thoughts that are more accurate, feel motivated to seek appropriate treatment and support, and **utilize the power of spirituality in your life**. I refer to treating pain responsibly as *Soul-Accounting*. It is worth every bit of your attention, focus, and patience.

You may discover through your fact-finding experiences that your own efforts are not sufficient and new strategies are needed. Since some triggers are deeply rooted, complex, and especially resistant, your efforts alone may be ineffective. Seek ***competent*** professional and spiritual help. There are many wonderful resources. You are not alone.

"...THE WISDOM TO KNOW THE DIFFERENCE". THE POWER OF THOUGHTS AND THE FORCE OF HABIT.

There are some experiences of pain that you can do nothing about. It just is, and the best intervention is to honor it and create a space for it in your heart. It is analogous to treating a physically wounded person. In such a case, you would prepare a clean, comfortable room for them, provide what they need, and then just give them the time and space to recover. However, there is some emotional pain that you *do* have control over. That is the felt experience of pain generated by your thoughts, consciously and unconsciously, which intensifies existing pain. What follows is a discussion of this thought-generated pain and a proposed strategy for dealing with it. It is important to note that an understanding of your pain is predicated on understanding the relationship between self-love and supervising your own thought process.

You can immediately begin to help yourself by setting up a mental boundary-filter. From this moment on, commit to being careful with what you let in and out of your mind, by guarding your thoughts. **Imagine that your mind is a vault with rare diamonds.** You seek to increase your diamond collection (truthful thoughts), but also have to take great care not to let any thieves come in and steal your precious jewels (peace of mind). By using a mental boundary-filter, you inspect each thought before it can get inside you and take up active residence.

There are four stages before a thought comes alive and takes on a life of its own. **Stage One** is when you have a sudden or unexpected thought. You give in to this thought. (A filter would not allow a potentially harmful thought to get past the Gates of Inspection to hurt you). **Stage Two** is indulging in these thoughts. **Stage Three** is where you display your thoughts either verbally or by the actions you take. **Stage Four** is indicated by self-destructive or otherwise unhealthy behaviors.

EXERCISE FOR WHEN TRAUMA-TRIGGERS ARE ACTIVATED

Think to a time when you acted in a way you later regretted. Plug in the whole process using these four stages.

Stage One: You give in to your unexpected thought. (No filter to keep out potentially harmful thoughts).	**Stage Two:** You indulge in these thoughts.	**Stage Three:** You display your thoughts either verbally or behaviorally.	**Stage Four:** Your respond with self-destructive or unhealthy behaviors.

Can you see how you had the opportunity to prevent self-harm only during stages one through three? If you are conscious of a thought you know *will* lead you down a dark road, discipline yourself to be quick in replacing those thoughts with ones that are truthful and compassionate. Say and practice any slogan that includes both of these spiritual principles. You want to eradicate the thought that was just starting to bud in your mind. **You must go to any length to protect your diamond vault (your mind and serenity)!**

EXERCISE IN SETTING UP MIND-FILTERS

Using the following sample chart, consider the same situation you detailed above, and the potential outcome, had you filtered your trigger before acting on it.

Trauma and Transformation: A 12-Step Guide.

My Trigger	My Reaction	My New Statement

Survivors are often plagued with thoughts of self-blame, self-hatred, excessive guilt and fear, and various counterproductive and pain producing thoughts. It is therefore critical that you do not ignore the need to monitor the thoughts, ideas, or suggestions that are involved with your pain cycles. The other areas of managing emotional pain include the discipline and devotion to self-care, a loving and safe support network, sufficient socialization, competent professional and spiritual counsel, and a consistent and genuine spiritual practice of your choosing.

Let us look further into this. Reflect on the last time you had that sinking feeling that seemed to come out of nowhere. Can you pinpoint the thought you had right before that feeling came upon you? If you cannot, try and pay attention the next time this happens, being especially mindful to note the fleeing, transitory thought that preceded it. Perhaps you can see the connection between that thought (that you may not have been aware that you had), and that sinking feeling. When you pay attention to your thoughts, also make note of which thoughts are truthful statements, and which are not. (**HINT: False statements and beliefs will always create pain, and contribute to existing pain**.) When you train yourself to make truthful statements to yourself, you open the door for the pain to breathe. Your 'pain breathing' can be felt as grief, which is an honor-ritual for its unmarked grave inside of you.

When you take control of the aspects of your pain that is self-generated by your thoughts, you are actively involved in fortifying those areas in your heart and psyche that are wounded, lost, alone, and confused. It will not just fortify them, but hopefully, the pain will slowly lessen and eventually turn into wisdom. Bear in mind that when you experience a bout of pain, and can identify what was the first conscious thought you had right before you experienced this pain, *you will see that the first thought you had is the most critical one.*

Another aspect to appreciate is the fire-power of habit. It is possible to be trapped by the dark side of pain which includes self-hatred, a vengeful spirit, and chronic anger. A survivor, who habitually allows himself to drown needlessly in such powerful, dark energies, can easily train themselves to think thoughts that generate hopeless feelings. This ultimately leads to a loss of hope in life. Sometimes this happens quickly, and sometimes this thinking corrodes the person's soul, slowly over an extended period of time. You may sink into a bottomless, dark well, having crossed the threshold of being able to exercise self-control.

Another powerful aspect of the force of habit is that you reach the point where you actively *believe* the negative self-thoughts, and identify them as the final truth about what happened. As you can well-imagine, this generates so much pain, because you are constantly reinforcing such lies to yourself. No one wants to hear, let alone, believe ongoing critical, messages being whispered in their ear. And yet, a survivor that tells himself lies (that he believes in), carries with him a never-ending whisper that feeds his pain, his hopelessness, and builds upon the layers of the already existing painful wound. From its genesis, habit of negative, untrue thought is powerful enough to deaden your true feelings and needs, especially your genuine need to grieve and mourn your losses.

RESPONSIBILITY-EXERCISE TOWARD YOUR PAIN

What I CAN do about my pain	What I CANNOT do about my pain	What is the responsible approach towards my pain?

You may be asking if it's possible for a survivor to reach the level of identifying *all* habitual thoughts that instigate pain, recognize the truth in each thought, and then being permanently free from it. The answer is that this is not an achievable goal nor is it necessary for healing. However, the objective is to reduce the intensity and frequency of the pain, as well as to practice healthy, spiritually-sound coping mechanisms as a lifestyle approach to having survived trauma. In addition, the objective includes accessing and utilizing loving, supportive people and whatever resources you require. This is predicated on the fundamental fact that a life based on personal meaning, truth, and grounded in reality, will make the pain **that you have no control over**, more easy to accept and tolerate.

Your role in supervising your thoughts is analogous to having a strand of diamonds. If you tie a knot at the further point, the diamonds will all stay on the strand. If you, the survivor, guard and nourish your thinking, you will strengthen your skill of monitoring your thoughts, and retain those thoughts that are truthful and life-affirming. However, there will be some pockets of pain within each person that can only experience healing through a connection with the Divine. Only you the survivor can identify what this means for you. Do not feel ashamed to ask for help, both from other appropriate people, and from your Higher Power. I am a staunch believer that every human being receives spiritual assistance as an equal match to their efforts.

Although the pain can feel excruciating, overwhelming, and without any end in sight, it is possible, through a regular practice, to free your mind from the nets and chains of negative habitual thinking. Rumi so eloquently put it: *"Ignore those that make you fearful and sad, that degrade you back towards disease and death."* This includes your own thoughts, perspective, and attitude.

Healing the pain requires a multitude of resources and quality support. In addition, your situation calls for *your* investment of significant patience and effort. You may need to take a slow, life-long journey, depending on your personal story and biology. Once the depths of your wound are explored, you can clearly differentiate which aspects of your wound you can directly influence and heal, and which corners of your wound remain untouchable. Every wound has a corner(s) sectioned off that remains "forbidden ground" and is better left to be healed by divine grace.

THE HEALING-WHEEL METHOD

The first step is to draw a pie-chart and identify your biggest triggers, slicing the pie according to the difficulty you have with each unresolved issue. You may even want to color-code each one, with that color representing the emotions that this trigger awakens in you. Below the chart, write a verse that most accurately describes your experience with it. For the upcoming week, one day at a time, monitor yourself for these triggers. Every time you experience one of these triggers put a little mark near that slice of your wheel. At the end of the week, carefully review all your triggers, so that you grasp what are your greatest areas of difficulty. For the upcoming week, re-write this same wheel with all the same details, except you are going to add rows on the bottom that refer to each trigger answering the following: *"What thought or action am I willing to replace this with?"* Every time you are triggered, intensely focus on the words that represent your new commitment. For example, if your moody cousin awakens your aggression, and you have engaged in altercations with him which leave you feeling exhausted, shaken and hurt, write the following as your new phrase every time you see him or think of him: *"I choose to disengage"*. The word *"disengage"* will be your code-word that you say to yourself as soon as you begin to feel triggered. I suggest you do this until it becomes your new habit.

Trauma and Transformation: A 12-Step Guide.

WEEK ONE

DRAW A PIE CHART, DIVIDING IT INTO SEGMENTS WITH CATEGORIES SUCH AS: PHYSICAL TRIGGER, HISTORICAL, EMOTIONAL, SOCIAL, AND FAMILY.

Use the following examples to help you record your triggers.

1. Whenever I visit my cousin John, I feel angry and resentful because he mistreats me. (Family)
2. When I am not acknowledged in a business meeting, I feel worthless. (Social)
3. Every time my mother says "no" to a request of mine, I want to break a vase. (Emotional)
4. When a boss looks at me disapprovingly, I feel annihilation anxiety. (Historical)
5. When I feel a migraine coming on, I simultaneously have a panic-attack that spirals out of control. (Physical)

WEEK TWO

DRAW A PIE CHART, DIVIDING IT INTO SEGMENTS WITH CATEGORIES SUCH AS: PHYSICAL TRIGGER, HISTORICAL, EMOTIONAL, SOCIAL, AND FAMILY.

1. *"I choose to disengage"*. <u>Disengage.</u>
2. *"I choose to remind myself that I am valuable"*.
   <u>Reminder: I am valuable.</u>
3. *"I am mindful with how I react to my feelings"*. <u>Mindful.</u>
4. *"I use intense responses to extend compassion to myself"*.
   <u>Compassion.</u>
5. *"I am willing to explore this physical reaction with self-love"*. <u>Self-Love.</u>

When seeking to develop a new habit, it is critical to set your intention in the form of a prayer, affirmation, or anything that is symbolic of your intention. Consider what your plans are for the day, including if you will encounter any situations that may be particularly triggering for you. If necessary, plan ahead and prepare yourself to handle that situation, if you cannot or should not avoid it. At night, review your wheel, your personalized statements, and responses. If you responded to a trigger in a way that you are regretful about, even partially, reflect why this took place. Were you overly fearful, reacted compulsively or made a mistake? Review your chart and use it as a tool for learning and growth.

Doing this daily will increase your level of awareness, which is an important first step in evaluating what areas you need help with. In addition, this daily practice is important to strengthen the force of habit. If applied consistently, it will help you in responding differently, which is connected to the intensity of your pain. This happens slowly, week by week, month by month and year by year, coupled with various additional tools, support, prayer and meditation. As the Jewish saying goes: *"A person is led in the direction he wants to go"*, so have confidence that your efforts will pay off! As time goes on and you find that your listed triggers are no longer a roadblock for you, they can be removed from the list and substituted with another, more troublesome trigger.

I suggest that you retain your charts and regularly analyze them, in order to monitor your growth or decline. **_Be mindful to address your triggers with extra care, sensitivity and empathy. The conditions in which triggers are created are always unpleasant ones._** I also suggest that you record the new insights you gain when you review your week. You may not always feel that you are progressing or accomplishing anything by doing this, and that "*it's the same old thing, so what?*" If this is your approach, the following tips may help boost your confidence and motivation:

HELPFUL SUGGESTIONS

1) Two are better than one: Seek a trustworthy and honest person with whom you can consult with.

2) Your spiritual life is a powerful source of energy and strength. It is directly related to your vitality and sense of

meaning in life. Therefore, it is important that you nourish your soul. This includes daily prayer, meditation, study, and distancing from dishonest, unkind people.

3) Not every suggestion or path will be a fit for each person, and there are as many difficulties as there are solutions. I have provided different suggestions, some which may not be useful for you. Each survivor should thoughtfully select that which she finds appropriate. Whatever you choose, I implore you **_NOT_** to choose to do nothing at all! The pain of trauma can be a serious block in your emotional and spiritual arteries. In the human body, such blockages can cause a significant weakening or death to the body. With the psyche, it is no different. Even the strongest person can fall weak to powerful triggers. Set aside a specific time, each day, to review and reflect. You are well-worth the quiet, meditative time for your serenity and well-being.

4) The more you act out on your triggers, the more you strengthen them. This is how humans are conditioned; reward, punishment, and reinforcement.

5) Even if you think that your heart forgot her pain (because you are numb, dissociated from your story and feelings, or do not think it matters), your pain is not released from your soul. Unprocessed suffering always leaves a trace inside of you. Every time you feel pain and you do not address it in a responsible way, this pain leaves a trace that combines itself with each new bout of pain, adding to the intensity. You keep remembering, even though you told yourself that you "forgot" or that "it doesn't matter". Obviously, the more intensely you experience pain, the more intense was the original event that created this trigger. It is important to pay attention to the degree and frequency that you experience such pain and in what areas of your life you feel it the most. Those areas are the most significant; both in pain and in growth potentiating.

6) If your mind is settled enough to explore your pain, your triggers, and to seek healing, it is worth your time and effort to do so. Your heart will patiently and quietly stand guard, as you go forth and seek the light which your mind, body and soul *need*. However, if your mind is too agitated, too fearful or you scorn your own suffering, your inner life may feel like a fearful darkness and weakness, void of strength and counsel. The wounded part of you is forsaken as it wanders through life dazed in its distress, descending into weariness and you become a victim of an illness that grabs hold of you, casting you into a deep dark pit.

7) Usually when you are in activation mode, you will react with either "fight" or "flight". You can feel totally unnerved, consumed with fear, and see your 'trigger' as your enemy. If you are seized with fright, you feel immobilized and can easily fall prey to the compulsion of the moment. Alternatively, you can be so consumed with blinding rage or feel the need to defend

yourself, and engage in an altercation that can easily be avoided. Have awareness into your nature, and act responsibly with your fears, triggers, and sensitivities.

8) The treatment can be more damaging than the illness. Be discerning in how you handle your emotional life. There are NO quick-fixes, magic cures, instant solutions, get-healthy-fast solutions. Your personal healing process is like a huge, colorful wheel. Each part of the cycle or wheel is affecting the other. What you think is irrelevant, "in the past", or in the closet of your memory, are all part of the complex web of interconnection and are linked together in numerous ways. Some are seen and some are waiting to be explored by you.

9) If your pain is chronic and feels more intolerable than death itself, act responsibly and seek good professional help. You do not have to live this way. If you choose to self-medicate thereby desensitizing yourself, on some level you begin to harden and

your natural sensitivity disappears. What usually accompanies this experience is worry and fear. These feelings spur the survivor to avoid the beginning of pain. He does this by moving away from the path of these powerful feelings so that it cannot strike him at all, or he chokes the pain at its source before it becomes real. This can be seen in active addicts, who often describe their motivation to use as filling the need "to numb out". Despite all his efforts, he sometimes finds himself suffering from pain which comes upon him suddenly. He suddenly remembers what once stung the depths of his soul. Since we are wired to avoid pain and seek pleasure, it is a natural instinct to seek to dull the pain of the soul. Developing tolerance to your pain, in conjunction with appropriate support and self-soothing techniques, will take you much further than the immediate gratification of numbing out in the moment. Just ask anyone who has successfully gone through this healing process.

10) You may have people in your life that are *"crazy-makers"*. If you do, and you can walk away from them, you may spare yourself a lot of ongoing and unnecessary aggravation. If you are able to, but choose not to walk away, you will end up influenced by them in some way. This can create unnecessary suffering from you and it can hinder your progress. Regardless, when you actively engage in "crazy-makers", you end up demeaning yourself. Self-esteem is built by doing esteem-able actions. Walking away from such people would qualify.

FINAL THOUGHTS

Practicing patience is critical to the process of healing your intense pain, reducing the intensity of your triggers, and choosing healthy responses when triggered. It can be likened to a person who is recovering from an illness or operation, and must take caution not to undo the effects of the treatment, **for as long as it takes.** As hard as it may be for the person, without patience, they can do serious damage to themselves. So too, a survivor who has made strides in lessening a trigger must be exceedingly careful in that area, even after they no longer experience significant interference with it.

If you incorporate this into your daily life, and learn from yourself, you will gain an increased level of awareness, self-compassion, more emotional freedom, true understanding and knowledge. Combined with the right action, you may experience the lessening of pain and an increase in genuine joy. And finally, you may be prone to feelings of regret over the past, and how you dealt with various situations. We are not prophets. If you did the best you could and did not act in deliberate vengeance allow yourself the gift of understanding. Look back at those times you regret, identify why you feel regret, and resort to a newfound commitment to growth, healing, and service to humanity.

If you are anything like me, you may feel sadness at the conclusion of a book that touched you. I would react this way and wish I could take the author with me wherever I went. When a book touched me, it touched upon my soul and I felt awakened and more hopeful. Some authors would end their book with saying "*I love you*", or "*I am with you in spirit even though I cannot be with you in person*". And being the highly sensitive soul that I am, I would cry. So here are my final thoughts to you. If you have been touched, awakened, or more curious after reading this book, you may be seeking help and are ready to receive it. As the saying goes "*When the student is ready, the Teacher appears.*" Your teacher can appear in various forms, just like your angels, including a book that comes your way.

I am with you in spirit because on some mysterious level, all of us *are* connected. Perhaps one day our paths will cross and we will connect in person. However, if that does not occur, I want you to hold on to the most important wisdom imparted to me: a loving Higher Power *always* responds to a genuine cry for help. It does not matter who or where you are. If your words are from your heart, you *are* being heard. The answers you receive, or the way things work out for you, may be unlike your fantasies or prayers. That is a good thing, because you may well be short-changing yourself. I have numerous personal examples of this, and have said many "thank-you" prayers for those situations.

When times get rough for you and you feel all alone, take a moment and close your eyes. Think of how precious you are. Think of every single survivor on a path of healing, holding a candle and facing you in a circle with you in the middle. Together we are all softly chanting your name, as we pray for your healing: mind, body, and soul. Please take us all with you, and when you are ready, pass along this vital message. Good luck on your journey!

Trauma and Transformation: A 12-Step Guide.

Biography of the Author

Rivka Edery, L.M.S.W. is a resident of Brooklyn, New York since 1994, and a native of Montreal, Canada. She has a Bachelor's of Arts in Social Science and a Masters in Social Work from Fordham University Graduate School of Social Service. She is a licensed social worker and a first time author specializing in trauma recovery and spirituality. She has been active in the treatment and recovery field for more than sixteen years. Since 2009, she has been working as a clinical social worker assisting clients who are recovering from trauma-related disorders. She has treated numerous clients and has talked with hundreds of recovering addicts. She is currently employed as a social work supervisor of a large residential drug treatment program. As her career was advancing, Rivka wondered if the ancient spiritual principles of the Twelve Steps of Alcoholics Anonymous can be applied to the healing of trauma. One day, she was suddenly inspired with an idea that had a firm hold on her and has not let go since. It combined the Twelve Steps of Alcoholics Anonymous that saved her life, with life problems that are a result of surviving traumatic experiences. The result is a unique approach for trauma survivors who are seeking a combined spiritual and clinical approach to their personal effects of surviving trauma.

To contact Ms. Edery for speaking or consulting, please call or e-mail
Tel: (646) 691-7771
Email: info@rivkaedery.com
Website: http://www.rivkaedery.com/default.html

REFERENCES

Alcoholics Anonymous, 3rd edition, New York: Alcoholics Anonymous World Services, Inc., 1976. (The "Big Book."), 59-60, 86, 164.

Twelve Steps and Twelve Traditions, New York: Alcoholics Anonymous World Services, Inc., 1981. (The "Twelve and Twelve."), 41, 98.

Chodron, Pema. *When Things Fall Apart: Heart Advice for Difficult Times.* Boston, MA: Shambhala Publications, Inc. Horticultural Hall, 1997, 164.

Dooley, Mike. *Choose Them Wisely Thoughts Become Things!* Hillsboro, Oregon: Atria Books/Beyond Words Publishing, Inc., 2009, 51.

Gibran, Kahlil. *The Treasured Writings of Kahlil Gibran*, New York: Castle Books, 2010, 57, 784, 786, 814, 834.

Keyes, Jr. Ken. *Gathering Power Through Insight and Love.* Coos Bay, Oregon: Living Love Publications, 1987, 148.

Levine, Ph.D. Peter A. *Healing Trauma.* Boulder, CO: Sounds True, Inc., 2008.

Prochaska, James O.; DiClemente, Carlo C. *Transtheoretical therapy: Toward a more integrative model of change.* Psychotherapy: Theory, Research & Practice, Vol 19(3), 1982, 276-288.

Rich, Adrienne, *On Lies, Secrets & Silence: Selected Prose 1966-1978.* (New York: Norton, 1979), 183-84.

Printed in Great Britain
by Amazon.co.uk, Ltd.,
Marston Gate.